Best Hikes Pittsburgh

The Greatest Views, Wildlife, and Forest Strolls

SECOND EDITION

Bob Frye

FALCONGUIDES

GUILFORD, CONNECTICUT

To Mom and Dad,
for all their support over the years

FALCONGUIDES®

An imprint of The Rowman & Littlefield Publishing Group, Inc.
4501 Forbes Blvd., Ste. 200
Lanham, MD 20706
www.rowman.com

Falcon and FalconGuides are registered trademarks and Make Adventure Your Story is a trademark of The Rowman & Littlefield Publishing Group, Inc.

Distributed by NATIONAL BOOK NETWORK
Copyright © 2018 The Rowman & Littlefield Publishing Group, Inc
A previous edition of this book was published by Falcon Publishing, Inc., in 2009.
All photos by Bob Frye unless otherwise noted
Maps by Ryan Mitchell © The Rowman & Littlefield Publishing Group, Inc.

British Library Cataloguing-in-Publication Information available

Library of Congress Cataloging-in-Publication Information available

ISBN 978-1-4930-3681-3 (paperback)
ISBN 978-1-4930-3682-0 (e-book)

∞™ The paper used in this publication meets the minimum requirements of American National Standard for Information Sciences—Permanence of Paper for Printed Library Materials, ANSI / NISO Z39.48-1992.

Printed in the United States of America

The author and The Rowman & Littlefield Publishing Group, Inc., assume no liability for accidents happening to, or injuries sustained by, readers who engage in the activities described in this book.

Contents

Overview

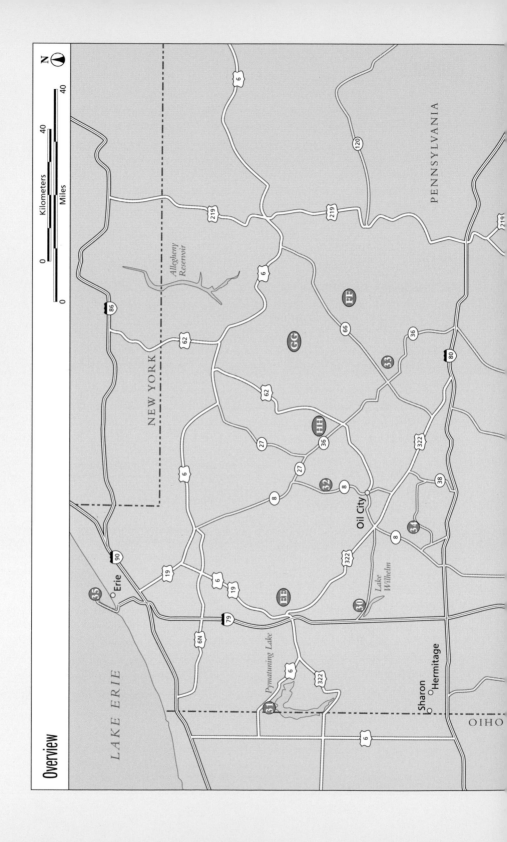

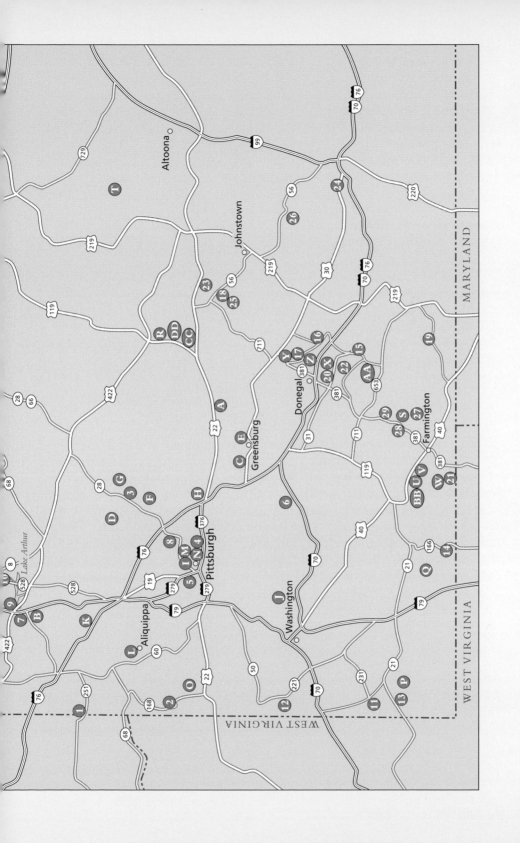

Acknowledgments

The Pittsburgh region and the greater expanse of western Pennsylvania have been blessed with some wonderful natural resources. It's our trails that most often allow us to see them up close. They wouldn't exist without the work of quite a few people, though.

I'd like to thank all of those trail volunteers who give up weekends to saw through blowdowns, build bridges, and map routes for the rest of us. We rarely see you, but your work is appreciated.

The people who work for our natural resource agencies deserve a hand, too. State park and forest crews, county and city park workers, and those who work for federal agencies like the National Park Service sink a lot of effort into trail work. Often they do it with budgets too small to cover needs, but they find a way.

Deserving of thanks as well is the Pennsylvania Game Commission. Funded almost solely by the sale of hunting licenses—it gets no general tax revenue—the commission buys and maintains game lands, primarily for the sake of sportsmen and wildlife. But hikers, bikers, birders, and others who never pick up a firearm have always been allowed to use its game lands free of charge, too. For all of those miles and acres open to everyone, thank you.

Finally, I'd like to thank God for providing our wonderful fields and forests and my family for giving me the freedom to get out and explore it all.

◀ *A view of Laurel Hill Creek as it enters Laurel Hill Lake downstream of Park Road.*

How to Use This Book

This book has been structured to aid you in determining which trails you might most like to hike. First the trails have been broken into four groups: those within the Pittsburgh Low Plateau; the Waynesburg Hills; the Allegheny Mountains; and those to the north of Pittsburgh.

Each chapter identifies a hike by name, gives a brief summary of what it's like, and identifies its starting point, length, approximate time needed to walk it, surface, and difficulty. We tell you, too, whether it's OK to take a dog along and what the rules are if you do, who else you might see on the trail, and in which seasons the hiking is best.

Also detailed is who owns the land, when it's open, and who to contact for more information. You also get a map with each chapter. These maps are not meant to replace topographic maps, road maps, and the detailed maps you can sometimes get from the landowners. They do, however, give you an inkling of what each trail is like.

Finally, and perhaps most importantly, each chapter gives a detailed description of the hike, with turn-by-turn directions and details on what you might see along the way, be it wildlife, historical sites, rock formations, or interesting flowers and trees.

Slippery Rock Creek is marked by lots of large boulders and rocks.

Introduction

Pittsburgh is the city that got cheated of a title.

At the dawn of the twentieth century, no one rated cities based on how dirty they were. On how much soot was in their air. On how grimy, gloomy, and utterly soiled they were. If they had, Pittsburgh would have won—blackened, scarred, calloused hands down.

Filth, thy champion was Pittsburgh.

Things were so bad that when Boston writer James Parton visited the city in 1868, he described it as "hell with the lid off." It was an apt description. The fires of heavy industry burned in the city like a mad rage in the eyes of a gluttonous dragon, devouring the surrounding countryside without pause. Night and day, rivers were defiled, mountains were debased, and the people who lived here were left to suffer the consequences.

One famous recollection of the city is how Pittsburghers had to leave their lights on all day, even at noon, because the smoke, dirt, and pollution in the air simply made it impossible to see otherwise.

Hikers walk out on rocks to explore the Youghiogheny River near Ferncliff Peninsula in Ohio-pyle State Park.

Happily, things are that way no more.

Pittsburgh has undergone a transformation. It was not an easy one. The death, or at least radical amputation, of the steel industry was an agonizing, decade-long bloodletting. Families built on paychecks from the mills—mine included to an extent, counting grandparents and uncles and in-laws—suffered enormously.

But the result has been a startlingly clean city and region. They sparkle now like a white diamond forged from black coal under enormous pressure. If you doubt that—if you're one of those who doesn't yet realize what the Pittsburgh and western Pennsylvania of today are like—get outside and take a look around.

You want wildlife close to home? Take the bus to Pittsburgh's Riverview Park and you might see white-tailed deer roaming hillsides where once the only animals were inside the cages of a zoo. Wilderness? Follow the dirt roads to Quebec Run, south of the city, and you'll find beauty as rugged and wild as anywhere. History? Solitude? Nature programming? The area has hikes that offer them all.

That's perhaps the greatest thing about this region. If the old cliché that says "there's a little bit of something here for everyone" holds true for hikers anywhere, this is that place.

I know that. Born and raised in western Pennsylvania, I've spent a lifetime roaming its fields and forests, and the beauty of this place still stuns me at times. Some of the hikes in this book are old favorites of mine. Others are new. Without exception, I found something in each that made me stop and say, "Oh, wow."

Hopefully you'll be equally impressed with what you see out there.

Weather

Your opportunities to find something you might like are certainly many. Pennsylvania offers three- and in some cases four-season hiking. There are exceptions, of course, but you can generally count on mild spring temperatures arriving by April and Indian summer lasting until October or even November.

Winter is a little iffier. The mountains of the Laurel Highlands and the regions north of Pittsburgh get more rain, snow, and fog, and they get it earlier than the city itself does. The roads leading to trailheads in those places can sometimes be treacherous or even impassable. But some of the hikes within the city and to the south and west can be done year-round. And if you're willing to walk in snowshoes, almost anything's possible.

Flora and Fauna

Much of western Pennsylvania is covered by what is known as Appalachian oak forest. It's dominated by white, red, and chestnut oaks; hickories; and white pines. Farther north, however, northern hardwood forests of hemlocks, black cherry, and American

◀ *Leaves frame the reflection of trees in a mud puddle along this Buffalo Creek hike.*

A group of white-tailed deer watch as hikers go by at Riverview Park.

beech are more common. The western edge of the state offers more sugar maple, black walnut, and basswood, while the southernmost tip gives you the chance to walk under the leaves of species that are relatively rare north of the Mason-Dixon Line, like yellow buckeye.

Pennsylvania's wildlife is equally rich and diverse. White-tailed deer; predators like black bears, coyotes, fishers, and bobcats; porcupines; bald eagles and ospreys; endangered rattlesnakes; and brook trout, bass, and catfish all live here.

Land Managers

Who owns the land on which all that flora and fauna thrive? The land is managed by a multitude of agencies, each with different goals—and accordingly different levels of devotion to the needs of hikers.

State parks offer a good network of trails, although some are of the shorter variety. If you want a longer walk, you often have to combine a few trails. That's not always bad, though. If you want to combine a hike with a picnic at a place that offers tables, primitive restrooms, and charcoal grills, these are good bets.

State forests are home to some of the state's longer hiking trails. Don't come expecting to be pampered, though. Amenities here are comparatively few. But if all you need is a place to park, a blazed trail, and some solitude, there is some real beauty to be had.

With a few exceptions, state game lands don't have much in the way of "official" hiking trails. That's because these lands were bought and are maintained with money generated by the sale of hunting licenses. If you don't hunt, you don't add acres to the game lands system or take care of what already exists. As stated earlier, the Pennsylvania Game Commission gets no general tax money. Understandably, these lands are managed primarily for hunters and wildlife. Hikers can and do make heavy use of them, however, in between hunting seasons.

City and county parks are like state parks in the sense that they try to serve the greatest variety of people. That means trails often get neither more nor less attention than playgrounds, soccer fields, and horseshoe pits. Some excellent trails do exist, however, and they're often the closest refuges to the city's center.

Is all of that enough to convince you to get outside and try walking your way around western Pennsylvania? I certainly hope so. This is a wonderful place to live, work, and play—especially play.

But don't take my word for it. Pick a trail and take off. You'll be glad you did.

Getting Around

Area Codes

The 412 area code services the city of Pittsburgh and some surrounding communities, taking in most of Allegheny County. The area code for the remainder of southwestern Pennsylvania is 724. The northwestern corner of Pennsylvania uses the 814 area code.

An informational kiosk on the north end of the Laurel Highlands Hiking Trail, leading to the Conemaugh Gap.

Roads

The Pennsylvania Department of Transportation offers information on road conditions on its website, www.511pa.com. It details weather conditions and alerts, possible traffic delays, weather forecasts, cameras, and more. Visitors to the site can also download a free app that offers audible travel alerts so you can listen while focusing on driving.

By Air

Pittsburgh International Airport is located on Route 60, just 16 miles west of downtown Pittsburgh. It is served by more than twenty passenger carrier airlines. Eight rental car companies are based at the airport, and public transportation, charter buses, taxis, and shuttles are available. For information call (412) 472-3525 or visit www.flypittsburgh.com.

The nearby Allegheny County airport handles a lot of traffic, too. In fact, it's the fifth-busiest airport in the state. Call (412) 461-4300.

By Rail

Pittsburgh is serviced via rail by Amtrak, which has a station in downtown. Several other stations are located in outlying communities, such as Greensburg and Latrobe. Call toll-free (800) 872-7245 or (412) 471-6171, or visit www.amtrak.com.

By Bus

Greyhound makes regular trips to and from Pittsburgh and surrounding communities. Call (412) 392-6256 or visit www.greyhound.com for information.

The Port Authority of Allegheny County provides bus transportation throughout Pittsburgh and Allegheny County. Call (412) 442-2000 or visit www.portauthority.org.

Visitor Information

Visit Pittsburgh is the official tourist promotion agency for Pittsburgh and surrounding Allegheny County. For information call (412) 281-7711 or visit www.visitpittsburgh.com.

For information on visiting the Laurel Highlands area, call (724) 238-5661 or toll-free (800) 333-5661, or visit www.laurelhighlands.com.

For details on visitor information for other parts of the state, contact the Pennsylvania Tourism Office toll-free at (800) 847-4872 or visit www.visitpa.com.

◄ *Hillside Trail where it bisects Pointer Rock Road and Nedrow Trail in Roaring Run Natural Area.*

Map Legend

Transportation

≡⟨80⟩≡   Freeway/Interstate Highway

=⟨101⟩=   US Highway

=⟨1⟩=   State Highway

=⟨1431⟩=   Other Road

= = =:   Unpaved Road

⊢—⊢—⊢   Railroad

Trails

▬▬▬▬   Selected Route

- - - - -   Trail or Fire Road

⟶   Direction of Travel

Water Features

◯   Body of Water

⤵ ⤵   Marsh/Swamp

〜   River or Creek

≋   Waterfalls

○⌐   Spring

Symbols

🄴   Trailhead

■   Building/Point of Interest

▲   Campground

⚑   Gate

⛯   Lighthouse

❓   Information Center

🅿   Parking

🜨   Fire Tower

🎴   Picnic Area

🚻   Restroom

◉   Scenic View

○   Towns and Cities

‿   Bridge

▥   Steps

N ⬆   True North (Magnetic North is approximately 15.5° East)

Land Management

▮   Local and State Parks

▮   State Forests

⬚   Natural Area

◀ *The covered bridge at the trailhead in Mingo Creek Park.*

Trail Finder

Hike No.	Hike Name	Best Hikes for Waterfalls	Best Hikes for Views	Best Hikes for Solitude
1	North Country Trail			•
2	Raccoon Creek State Park			
3	Harrison Hills Park			
4	Frick Park			
5	Riverview Park			
6	Youghiogheny River Trail			
7	Slippery Rock Gorge	•		
8	Beechwood Farms Nature Reserve			
9	Glacier Ridge Trail			•
10	Jennings Environmental Education Center			
11	Mingo Creek	•		
12	Buffalo Creek			
13	Ryerson Station State Park		•	
14	Friendship Hill National Historic Site			
15	Laurel Hill State Park	•		
16	Wolf Rocks Trail		•	
17	Grove Run Trail	•		
18	Conemaugh Gap		•	
19	Mount Davis		•	
20	Mountain Streams			
21	Quebec Run Wild Area	•		•
22	Roaring Run Natural Area	•		•
23	Charles F. Lewis Natural Area			•
24	Shawnee State Park			
25	New Florence		•	
26	John P. Saylor Trail			•
27	Ohiopyle's Sugarloaf-Baughman Loop		•	
28	Ohiopyle's Ferncliff Peninsula	•		
29	Bear Run Nature Reserve		•	
30	Maurice K. Goddard State Park			
31	Pymatuning State Park			•
32	Petroleum Center			
33	Cook Forest State Park		•	
34	Allegheny Gorge		•	
35	Presque Isle			

Best Hikes for Children	Best Hikes for Back-packers	Best Hikes for Streams and Rivers	Best Hikes for History Lovers	Best Hikes for Viewing Wildlife	Best Hikes for Lake Lovers	Best Hikes in Winter
	●				●	
		●			●	
●						●
●				●		●
		●				●
		●				
●				●		●
●				●		
●				●		●
●				●		●
			●			●
●			●	●		●
		●	●		●	
		●				
	●					
		●				
	●	●				
		●				
	●			●		
●				●	●	
				●		
	●					
		●				
	●					
●				●	●	●
				●	●	
	●	●	●			
		●				
			●			
					●	

The Pittsburgh Low Plateau

T he area of the state defined as the Pittsburgh Low Plateau dominates the western third of Pennsylvania. It stretches from the West Virginia border in the south three-quarters of the way north to the New York line and from the Ohio border in the west to nearly Pennsylvania's center in the east.

The ground here sits on a base of rock containing the bulk of the significant bituminous coal in Pennsylvania. Strip mines meant to harvest that coal have been and remain common. Some old strips look as they did when the miners packed up and left; others have been reclaimed. Still others are yet in operation.

The region features generally mild terrain—broad, undulating lowlands cut by numerous narrow, yet relatively shallow, valleys. Elevations range from 660 to 1,700 feet, but variations of more than 200 feet from one point to the next are relatively rare outside of some stream bottoms. More often, gentle slopes predominate.

With Pittsburgh at its core, this is the most populous area of western Pennsylvania in terms of people. Consequently, public land exists in smaller chunks than in other parts of Pennsylvania.

But that doesn't mean you can't escape to the outdoors here. From the rugged Slippery Rock Gorge to the bluffs above the Allegheny River in Harrison Hills Park to city parks seemingly within a stone's throw of downtown, there are numerous opportunities to get outside and put some miles on those boots. You'll want to take advantage of them.

◄ *Late afternoon sun hits the woods in Frick Park.*

1 North Country Trail

The North Country National Scenic Trail is a behemoth of a footpath, winding though seven states on its way from the eastern edge of New York to North Dakota. Pennsylvania ranks third in terms of the number of off-road trail miles established. This particular section takes you across state game lands to the Pennsylvania–Ohio border, where you can say you stood with one foot in each state.

Start: A small parking area where the North Country Trail crosses Watts Mill Road
Distance: 7.6 miles out and back
Approximate hiking time: 3.5–4 hours
Difficulty: Moderate to difficult, with a few climbs and narrow spots
Trail surface: Dirt paths and old roadways
Seasons: Year-round
Other trail users: Hunters (some, if disabled, on all-terrain vehicles) and cross-country skiers
Canine compatibility: Dogs permitted; leashes not required
Land status: State game lands
Fees and permits: No fees or permits required
Schedule: Game land open year-round, but this land was bought and is maintained using money from the sale of hunting licenses, so sportsmen have first use of the land. If you're planning to come here with an organized group, you need approval from the Pennsylvania Game Commission beforehand, particularly at certain times of year.
Maps: A map of State Game Lands 285, and a listing of game lands regulations, can be found at www.pgc.pa.gov/HuntTrap/StateGame Lands/Pages/default.aspx. USGS New Galilee
Trail contacts: Pennsylvania Game Commission, Southwest Region Office, 4820 Route 711, Bolivar 15923; (724) 238-9523; www .pgc.state.pa.us
Special considerations: This area is very popular with hunters, primarily from October through late January and again from late April to late May. If you want to hike here at those times of year, it's best to do so on Sunday, when most hunting is prohibited.

Finding the trailhead: From Pittsburgh follow US Highway 22/30 west and turn onto Route 60 north. You'll then get on Route 51 north and then Route 251 west, continuing until you come to a right turn onto Watts Mill Road. Follow Watts Mill for 2 miles and you'll see the signs where the trail crosses the road; there's very limited parking here. *DeLorme: Pennsylvania Atlas & Gazetteer:* Page 56 B2. Trailhead GPS coordinates: N40 47.398 / W80 29.368

The Hike

You can take the Pennsylvania Turnpike to reach Ohio. You can do the same with Interstate 70. Or you can get there by walking the North Country Trail across State Game Lands 285.

A trail that when completed will be the longest in the country—even surpassing the granddaddy of them all, the Appalachian Trail—the North Country Trail cuts diagonally across northwestern Pennsylvania from New York to Ohio.

The North County Trail stretches from New York to North Dakota, with 97 miles passing through Pennsylvania.

This particular section of the trail offers some nice views of Little Beaver Creek, an area where brick miners dug for the clay that kept them in business, and wildlife—all at considerably less than 65 miles per hour.

It enters the game lands rather inconspicuously. A sign along Watts Mill Road notes that it's a 3.8-mile walk to the Ohio border, but with limited parking available, you'll never find crowds at this launch point.

The trail begins by following a hillside around until at 0.2 mile you come to an open swath. By looking to your right, you can see little Beaver Creek in the distance.

The North Country National Scenic Trail is the longest in the National Trails System, stretching 4,600 miles over seven states, from the middle of North Dakota to the Vermont–New York border. It passes through a national grassland, 10 national forests, more than 150 federal, state and local public lands, and through the Adirondacks, among other things. Visit www .northcountrytrail.org for more information.

A chipmunk, no doubt preparing for its winter hibernation, stuffs it cheeks along the North Country Trail.

The trail next passes some interesting rock formations at 0.5 mile. A few hundred yards farther the trail Ts; turn right to follow the trail's blue blazes and keep the edge of a field on your left.

You'll circle the field and come to its far edge at 0.8 mile, then enter a stretch of woods thick with hanging grapevines at 1.1 miles. A number of small but steep humps here look like mountains in miniature.

You get another view of the valley below at 1.4 miles. The forest here is very brushy. Mile 1.5 brings you to a T in the trail; turn left to continue following the blazes. More views of the hollow are offered as you follow the trail just below ridgeline.

Mile 2.4 brings you to a petroleum pipeline. Peek over its edge on the right for a sweeping view before turning left. You'll follow this pipeline for 0.1 mile, then turn right and climb a small hill. The trail circles around a field here. Notice the staghorn sumac—identifiable by its fuzzy stems and red cone-shaped flower—growing along the field's edge.

The trail follows the edge of the field for a while, then turns left to cross it. Posts marked with blue blazes in the field mark the way.

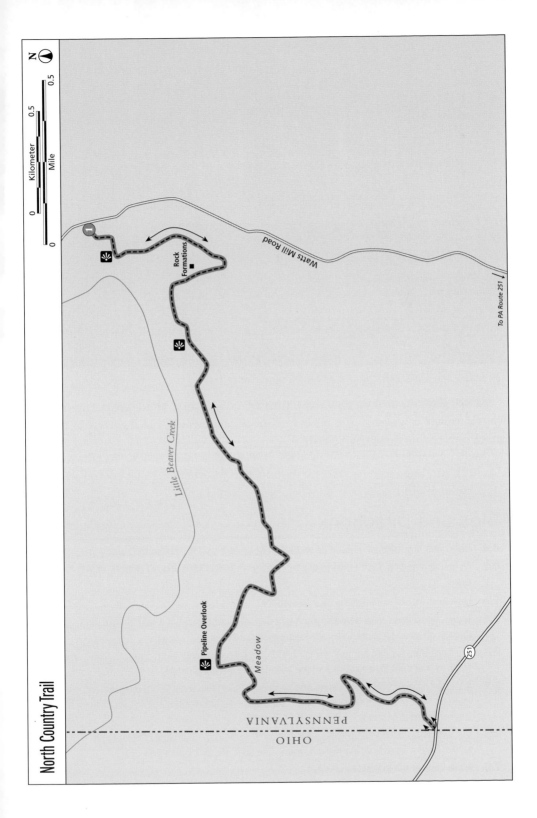

North Country Trail

The setting sun shines through trees on the North Country Trail.

At 3.1 miles the trail Ys; turn right. Turn left at another Y at 3.2 miles. The trail clings narrowly to the side of a hill before dropping downhill. You'll emerge at the Pennsylvania–Ohio border at 3.8 miles.

You'll turn and retrace your steps to the starting point here, but first cross the road and check out the concrete marker for the state line. It's crumbling a bit but still offers a nice backdrop for a picture to show where you ended up.

Miles and Directions

0.0 Begin at a tiny roadside pull-off on Watts Mill Road at a sign for the North Country Trail.

0.2 As you approach a slight curve to the left, look to your right for a view of Little Beaver Creek.

0.5 Look here for some interesting rock formations.

1.4 There's no "official" view here like you might find at some parks, but a look to your right through an opening in the trees provides a nice scenic view.

2.4 You'll climb up a slight hump in the trail and emerge onto a petroleum pipeline. Take a few steps to your right for a nice view of the valley below via the pipeline.

2.5 After turning right from the pipeline and climbing a short hill, you'll find a meadow on your left. Skirt this, keeping it on your left, for a while before crossing it. Look for distinctive staghorn sumac as you go.

3.8 The trail reaches the Pennsylvania-Ohio border. A somewhat crumbling concrete mile marker on the far side of the highway marks the spot. Retrace your steps.

7.6 Arrive back at the roadside pull-off.

2 Raccoon Creek State Park

Many of the casual visitors to Raccoon Creek State Park congregate in its eastern end, where 101-acre Raccoon Lake and most of the picnic areas are located. The western half of the park is not to be missed, though. Its network of trails winds though hardwood forests, past a wetland and pond, and along some interesting creek bottoms.

Start: The parking area at the junction of Route 168 and Nichol Road
Distance: 8.0-mile loop
Approximate hiking time: 3.5–4 hours
Difficulty: Moderate, with some wet spots
Trail surface: Dirt paths and unpaved roads
Seasons: Year-round
Other trail users: Horseback riders, cross-country skiers, bicyclists
Canine compatibility: Leashed dogs permitted
Land status: State park
Fees and permits: No fees or permits required

Maps: A map is available by contacting Raccoon Creek State Park. Trail maps, complete with contour lines, can also be downloaded at www.friendsofraccoon.com. USGS Hookstown
Trail contacts: Raccoon Creek State Park, 3000 State Route 18, Hookstown 15050-9416; (724) 899-2200; www.dcnr.state.pa.us/stateparks/parks/raccooncreek.aspx
Special considerations: Portions of this hike are through areas open to hunting. The hike also shares the trail with horses at points, so give them the right-of-way.

Finding the trailhead: Take Route 18 north to Frankfort Springs, then go north on Route 168 for 3.6 miles to Nichol Road. *DeLorme: Pennsylvania Atlas & Gazetteer:* Page 56 D1. Trailhead GPS coordinates: N40 31.286 / W80 28.888

The Hike

It's fitting that the triangular piece of private property bounded by Route 168, Nichol Road, and the boundary of Raccoon Creek State Park is home to horses. This end of the park sees quite a few of them, their riders traveling over trails with names like Appaloosa, Pinto, and Buckskin.

There's some wonderful walking here, too, though, even if you use your own two feet.

To begin, park in the lot at the gated end of Nichol Road. Follow the road for a little less than 500 feet, then turn left onto Appaloosa Trail. The going here might be on hard-packed dirt or clumpy mud with horseshoe-shaped divots, depending on the weather and the amount of use it has seen, but it's relatively easy going either way.

Bypass a turnoff for Heritage Trail at 0.5 mile and continue on Appaloosa through a mix of oaks and shagbark hickory. At 1.0 mile look for a cinder block foundation being reclaimed by nature, then a marker for the Appaloosa Spur Trail just a short while later. Ignore the marker and continue along Appaloosa Trail.

Trees are reflected in wind-dappled water of the Upper Pond in Raccoon Creek State Park.

Mile 1.9 brings you to a side trail leading to the Pioneer Backpacking Area. There are five shelters here and five tent sites (and five more of each off Forest Trail) spread over 19.5 miles of trail, if you care to make this into an overnighter or at least get some water or use the restroom.

Back on the trail, at 2.9 miles, just after passing a few walnut trees, Appaloosa Trail meets Nichol Road. Turn left, cross a bridge over Traverse Creek, and turn right when the road Ys 100 feet farther along. You're in the open here, but be alert for wildlife like squirrels, blue jays, and red-tailed hawks.

Look for a small waterfall at 3.1 miles, then make a right turn onto Wetlands Trail at 3.3 miles. This area can be wet, although logs, cut into disks and spaced on the trail like saucers, provide some dry footing.

This hike puts you back into the sun at 3.5 miles, when the trail leaves the woods to follow a grassy creek bottom. There's a field of cattails at 3.8 miles and then the park's Upper Pond. Watch here for turtles, bluegills and bass, and herons.

Go past the pond, ignoring a sign for Heron Trail, until Wetland Trail ends at a road at 4.5 miles. Turn right onto the road, cross a bridge, and turn left onto Camp Trail opposite a parking area and shed. In less than 0.1 mile you'll come to a Y; turn left onto a short connector trail, then right onto Heritage Trail 100 yards or so farther on.

This trail, marked with blue blazes, angles uphill away from a creek bottom. The forest is very diverse for the next mile or so. Some sections look almost manicured,

A look at the Upper Pond in Raccoon Creek State Park.

with very little in the way of understory. In other areas it's very dense, with lots of tree species regenerating.

You'll cross a power line at 6.2 miles and a road leading to the Linsly Outdoor Center at 6.4 miles. Mile 6.8 brings you to a bridge over a tiny trickle of a stream. The trail follows that creek, with some thicker growth crowding in on the trail's edges.

Cross another stream at 7.0 miles. Turn left, ignoring a trail that seems to wind away to the right, and continue to follow the blue blazes.

WILDFLOWER BONANZA

If you're going to visit Raccoon Creek State Park, leave yourself a little time to check out its wildflower reserve.

More than 700 species of plants—enough to rank this as perhaps the most diverse collection of wildflowers in the state—have been identified within its 314 acres. The peak of the bloom comes between late April and August, but you can find something flowering here much of the year. Information available at the reserve's interpretive center will tell you what to expect and when.

The reserve is closed to all activities but hiking, and pets are prohibited. Call the state park (724-899-2200) for information.

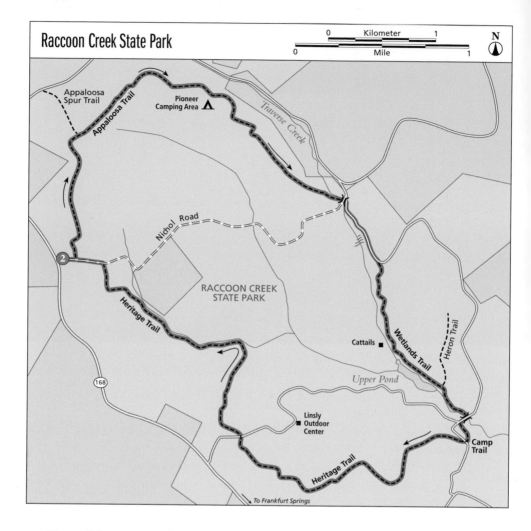

0   Kilometer   1

0   Mile   1

N

Appaloosa
Spur Trail

Appaloosa Trail

Pioneer
Camping Area

Traverse Creek

Nichol Road

2

Heritage Trail

RACCOON CREEK
STATE PARK

168

Cattails

Wetlands Trail

Heron Trail

Upper Pond

Linsly
Outdoor
Center

Camp
Trail

Heritage Trail

To Frankfurt Springs

The trail is serpentine here, winding back and forth across the creek several times. There are no bridges, but the stream is small enough to step across. You finally leave it behind at 7.4 miles, when the trail climbs out of the creek valley.

Heritage Trail crosses Nichol Road at 7.6 miles. Turn left here and follow the road back to your vehicle.

Miles and Directions

0.0   Start at the parking area on Nichol Road, going around the gate to follow the dirt-and-gravel roadway.

0.1   Travel a short way down Nichol Road and then—near a field that often has horses in it on the right—turn left onto Appaloosa Trail.

1.9   You'll pass a sign on your right for the Pioneer Backpacking Area, one of several places in the park where hikers can spend the night.

Many of the trails that wind through Raccoon Creek State Park are open to foot traffic only.

2.9 Appaloosa Trail comes to a T with Nichol Road. You'll go left, cross a small bridge, then turn right to stay on Nichol Road.

3.1 Look on your right for a small but pretty waterfall.

3.3 Turn off Nichol Road onto Wetlands Trail, being sure to keep an eye out for the sign here so that you don't miss it.

4.0 A wetlands full of cattails announces the upper end of the park's Upper Pond. Follow the trail and the pond becomes more evident as you go.

4.6 Turn left onto Camp Trail opposite a small parking lot and shed. If you start uphill on the paved road, you've gone too far.

6.2 Cross a power line where the trail next leads into some pines.

7.0 You'll find a tiny bridge here over an equally small stream.

7.6 Heritage Trail runs into Nichol Road. Turn left to follow the road back toward your car.

8.0 Arrive back at the parking area.

3 Harrison Hills Park

As hidden as any park can be in one of the state's most populous counties, Harrison Hills offers some wonderful scenery and some truly challenging walking. The eastern end of the Rachel Carson Trail—a 35.7-mile pathway across the county—begins here and when connected with some other park trails allows you to get in a good loop hike. Wildlife, particularly white-tailed deer, abounds here.

Start: The Wetlands Trail, at the parking lot on Chipmunk Road, where you turn to get to the park's maintenance office
Distance: 5.3-mile loop
Approximate hiking time: 2.5–3 hours
Difficulty: Moderate to difficult due to challenging climbs in some areas
Trail surface: Dirt paths, with some road crossings
Seasons: Year-round; some views best when the leaves are off the trees
Other trail users: Cross-country skiers
Canine compatibility: Leashed dogs permitted
Land status: Allegheny County park

Fees and permits: No fees or permits required
Schedule: Access to the parking area from daylight to dusk
Maps: Map available by contacting Harrison Hills Park; USGS Freeport
Trail contacts: Harrison Hills Park, 5200 Freeport Road, Natrona Heights 15065; (724) 295-3570; www.alleghenycounty.us/parks/hhfac.aspx
Special considerations: The portion of this hike that follows the Rachel Carson Trail has some serious drop-offs. Be especially careful with children here.

Finding the trailhead: Harrison Hills is located near Natrona Heights in the extreme northeastern corner of Allegheny County. From Pennsylvania Turnpike exit 48 in New Kensington, take Route 28 north toward New Kensington to exit 16, for Route 908 east. Turn right onto Millerstown Road, then right again onto Freeport Road. The park entrance will be on the left. The parking area is on Chipmunk Road. *DeLorme: Pennsylvania Atlas & Gazetteer:* Page 58 C1. Trailhead GPS coordinates: N40 39.318 / W79 42.235

The Hike

Despite having its share of playgrounds, picnic areas, restrooms, and other facilities, Harrison Hills Park is considered the "greenest"—i.e., least developed—of Allegheny County's parks. It has a very nice network of trails that are well blazed and easy to follow. They take you past some spectacular views of the Allegheny River and two ponds often full of waterfowl.

You won't have to battle big crowds, either. While this isn't wilderness by any means, the traffic here is light in comparison to what you might encounter while hiking the county's North and Boyce Parks, for example.

A view of the Allegheny River from an overlook in Harrison Hills Park. ▶

The trailhead at Harrison Hills Park.

Begin this hike on the green-blazed Wetlands Trail, which starts near the parking lot at the junction of Chipmunk Road and the unnamed road leading to the park maintenance office. Enter the woods on Wetlands Trail by crossing the road near a phone booth. In about 230 feet you'll connect with the red-blazed Scout Trail. Turn right, past the restrooms.

At 0.2 mile the Wetlands and Scout Trails split; turn right to stay on Scout. You'll cross a small bridge at 0.4 mile and then, at the crest of a small hill, turn left and then right at the fence surrounding the park's composting site. A red blaze painted on the blacktop marks the way.

THE RACHEL CARSON TRAIL

If you're looking for a real challenge, you can try doing the 35.7-mile Rachel Carson Trail—which stretches from one side of Allegheny County to the other—in one day.

The Rachel Carson Trails Conservancy sponsors an annual "Endurance Hike." Hikers are tasked with walking 34 miles of the trail end to end within one day.

That's definitely not easy. Aside from the sheer distance, most of the trail, outside of Harrison Hills and North Parks, runs across private property. It's steep in places and less than perfectly groomed in others.

For information visit the Rachel Carson Trails Conservancy online at www.rachelcarson trails.org or e-mail info@rachelcarsontrails.org.

Follow the field edge, then drop back into the woods until, at 0.6 mile, you'll find the river bluffs directly in front of you. A bench offers a place to sit. Ignore this for now and instead turn left to follow the red and green blazes again.

Mile 0.7 brings another Y in the trail; head right downslope through a hollow. Be aware of the poison ivy here.

You'll come to pond at 1.0 mile. Turn right and circle the pond. Red blazes are few here, but if you keep the pond on your left, you'll pick them up again on the right just before you reach the road.

Crossing a gravel road at 1.3 miles links the Scout and yellow-blazed Rachel Carson Trails. This is the most challenging yet most scenic part of the hike; it leads along the edge of the cliffs that rise high above the Allegheny. Look for the waterfalls that disappear over the edge of the bluffs.

You'll find some nice views of the river at 1.4, 1.7 (at the bench you passed earlier), and 2.4 miles, where there's a marker dedicated to Michael Watts, a Pittsburgh chemist who worked hard to improve local water quality.

At 2.7 miles you'll cross a small stream, climb a bank, and turn left when the trail Ts. About 0.25 mile farther, turn left again to follow the red blazes.

A hiker walks from the overlook of the Allegheny River at Harrison Hills Park.

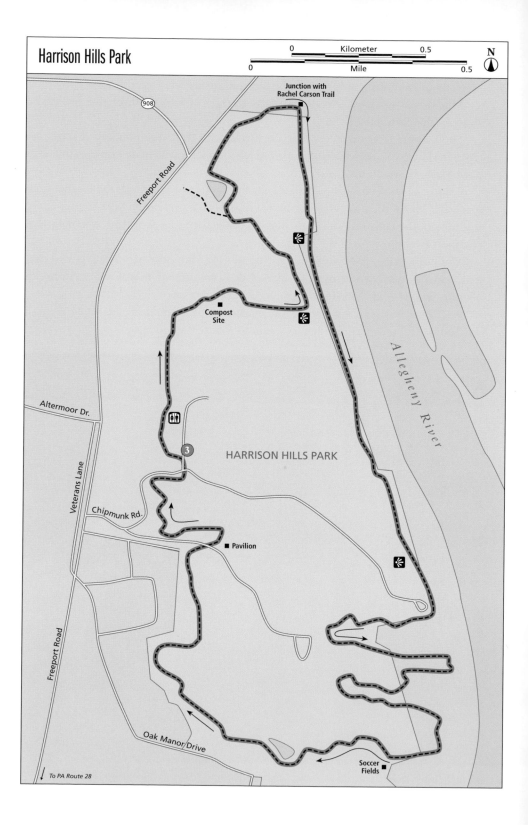

Harrison Hills Park

0   Kilometer   0.5

0   Mile   0.5

N

908

Junction with
Rachel Carson Trail

Freeport Road

Compost
Site

Allegheny River

Altermoor Dr.

3

HARRISON HILLS PARK

Veterans Lane

Chipmunk Rd.

Pavilion

Freeport Road

Oak Manor Drive

Soccer
Fields

To PA Route 28

The trail loops back toward the river here. Unfortunately you'll also see some danger signs posted around a section of woods littered with glass bottles, old cans, and other garbage. Heed the signs and stay out of this area.

Mile 3.1 brings you to another T; turn left, not on the road but where the red blazes lead. You'll loop back toward the river one last time until, at 3.5 miles, the trail emerges into a field. Angle toward the red-blazed post in its center. Turn left at a row of conifers, keeping a soccer field on your left and the concession stand on your right. The trail becomes obvious again at the far end of the field.

The park's second pond comes into view at 3.7 miles. Turn left at the pond, then right to keep the pond on your right. Pass a couple of benches, then climb a hill and reenter the woods. Turn left at the Y to stay with the red blazes. The trail will pass behind some houses here.

At 4.9 miles the trail meets the park road. Turn right on the road, then turn left by a picnic pavilion. The trail reenters the woods on the left just behind the pavilion.

The trail Ts one last time at 5.1 miles; turn right. At 5.2 miles the trail doubles back on itself to drop down to Chipmunk Road. Turn right and walk the road back to your vehicle.

Miles and Directions

0.0   Start at a parking lot near the Wetlands Trail.

0.2   Just beyond a restroom building, Wetlands and Scout Trails will split. Turn right onto Scout Trail.

0.4   The trail brings you face to face with a composting area. Turn left, keeping the composting area on your right.

1.0   The trail bypasses the first of two small ponds located within the park.

1.3   The trail, near a power line, meets the famous Rachel Carson Trail. Turn right to follow the Rachel Carson Trail.

2.4   This is the park's most well-developed overview of the Allegheny River and a good place to take pictures.

3.5   The trail leaves the woods to cut between some soccer fields. Keep the concession stand on your right.

3.7   Here you'll skirt the park's second pond, which is a good place to see waterfowl and occasionally deer.

4.9   The trail crosses a road and runs beside a picnic pavilion, a good place to stop for one last break before you're done.

5.3   Arrive back at the parking lot.

4 Frick Park

This loop hike through Frick Park involves a few hills, but it's relatively easy overall. Some of the sights you'll see are the tiny Hot Dog Dam, an even smaller pond, and, if you're lucky, people lawn bowling at the only site in Pennsylvania where that game still goes on. You'll pass a wetland as well. Expect to see lots of people, too.

Start: The Frick Environmental Center
Distance: 5.1-mile double loop
Approximate hiking time: 2.5–3 hours
Difficulty: Easy to moderate, with just a few climbs
Trail surface: Dirt paths
Seasons: Year-round
Other trail users: Cross-country skiers, bicyclists, and joggers
Canine compatibility: Dogs permitted but must be leashed outside designated off-leash areas
Land status: City park

Fees and permits: No fees or permits required
Maps: Map available by contacting Pittsburgh Parks and Recreation; USGS Pittsburgh East
Trail contacts: Pittsburgh Parks and Recreation, 414 Grant Street, Room 400, Pittsburgh 15219; (412) 255-2539; www.city.pittsburgh .pa.us/parks/index.html
Special considerations: Signs at the parking area warn you not to leave valuables in plain view on the seats of your car, as vandals have been a problem. If you're leaving something in your car, lock it in the trunk or hide it out of sight.

Finding the trailhead: From the Parkway West (Interstate 376), take exit 7 toward Edgewood/ Swissvale. Turn right onto South Braddock Avenue, left onto Forbes Avenue, and left onto South Dallas Avenue. Finally turn left onto Beechwood Boulevard. *DeLorme: Pennsylvania Atlas & Gazetteer:* Page 71 A6. Trailhead GPS coordinates: N40 26.172 / W79 54.408

The Hike

Many hikes take you through areas with few people. That's not the case at Frick. Despite being the largest of Pittsburgh's parks (600 acres), Frick is also often the busiest.

Walk here at any time and you'll find joggers, lawn bowlers, bicyclists, high school cross-country runners, skiers, and others. And that's just in the daytime. Head for your vehicle at dusk, thinking the day is done, and you'll often meet people who hike here at night, with headlamps for both themselves and their dogs.

It's a multicultural crowd, too; listen for a moment and you'll hear a variety of languages being spoken.

This hike begins on the South Clayton Loop Trail near the Frick Environmental Center (not to be confused with the Frick Art and Historical Society). It's not marked, but if you walk to the end of the parking area, keeping the composting area and Meadow Trail on your left, you'll find it by a water fountain.

A jogger, seen through some hanging leaves, runs along one of Frick Park's trails.

Walk a hundred yards or so and you'll pass the outdoor classroom and Nature Trail on your right. Bypass that trail for now—you'll return on it later.

Mile 0.4 brings you to an overlook marked by a split-rail fence. In another 0.1 mile you'll make a sharp right turn and head downhill on Biddle Trail. You'll next come to a four-way intersection with a fire hydrant in the middle of the woods. Turn left here onto Tranquil Trail.

This wide, flat stretch of trail follows Fern Hollow Creek. Cross under Forbes Avenue, past Hot Dog Dam on your right and a small pond on your left.

Mile 1.0 brings you to a Y in the trail; turn right (uphill) onto Homewood Trail. You'll get a nice view of the valley below and some sandstone on the right, particularly at an overlook with a bench. A few steps beyond this spot, make a sharp right turn onto Kensington Trail.

At a T at the top of this hill at 1.2 miles, make a 90-degree turn left onto Hawthorne Trail. You'll pass the lawn bowling club and, a few steps later, Frick Art and Historical Center.

Continue past a set of steps on the left to the Gatehouse at Reynolds Street, turning left near a cemetery onto Tranquil Trail again at 1.6 miles. Watch for squirrels here as they scamper around.

The entrance to the Frick Environmental Center.

Follow Tranquil Trail back past the turnoff for Homewood Trail. Notice just before this point that you get to see the overlook you were at before, this time from the bottom.

At the intersection with Biddle Trail, continue straight on Tranquil Trail. You'll turn right onto Falls Ravine Trail by a pavilion at 2.8 miles. This trail, which has a cathedral feel because of the tall trees that line it, goes uphill past some rock formations.

Follow Falls Ravine uphill to mile 3.2, then make a sharp left onto Lower Riverview Trail. The trail here winds through a younger forest.

Pass a sign on the left for Firelane Extension and reach a Y at 3.9 miles. Turn right onto Riverview Trail, which loops around and brings you to another Y at 4.6 miles. Turn right and go down the hill on Riverview Extension. (NOTE: Turning left would take you to another leash-free area for dog owners.)

At 4.8 miles you'll find yourself back at the spot where you first turned onto Lower Riverview. This time, turn left onto Ravine Trail and circle a gully until you come to a junction with Nature Trail at 4.9 miles. Turn right onto Nature Trail, keeping a large observation deck on your left.

In another 0.1 mile Nature Trail runs into South Clayton Loop. Turn left and walk back to the parking lot.

If you're interested in learning more about lawn bowling, the Frick Park Lawn Bowling Club is a wonderful resource. Information is available at www.lawnbowlingpittsburgh.org.

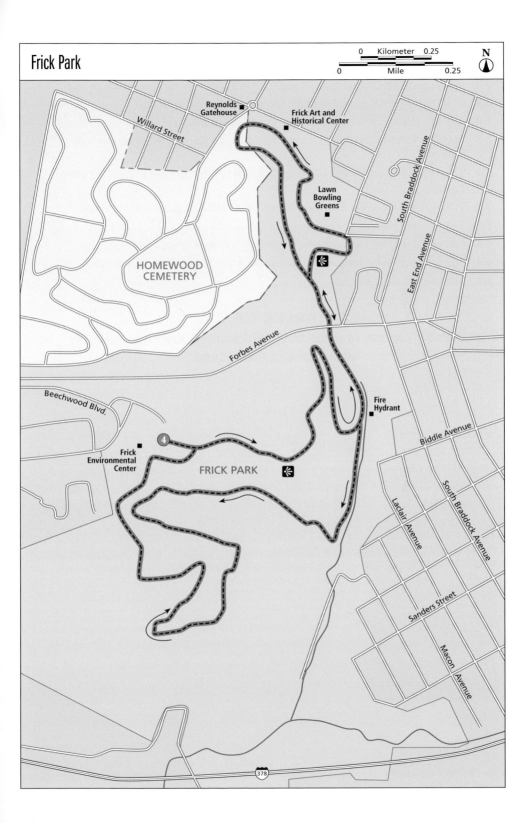

Frick Park

0   Kilometer   0.25

0   Mile   0.25

N

Willard Street

Reynolds Gatehouse

Frick Art and Historical Center

Lawn Bowling Greens

HOMEWOOD CEMETERY

Forbes Avenue

South Braddock Avenue

East End Avenue

Beechwood Blvd.

Fire Hydrant

Biddle Avenue

Frick Environmental Center

FRICK PARK

4

Ladlair Avenue

South Braddock Avenue

Sanders Street

Macon Avenue

378

Miles and Directions

0.0 Start at the South Clayton Loop trailhead, located a short walk from the parking lot.

0.4 Come to an overlook, marked by a split-rail fence on the right of the trail.

1.0 Turn right at a Y to climb Homewood Trail, which leads to a nice overlook.

1.5 Pass Frick Park Lawn Bowling Club, which has greens on your right where you may spot bowlers.

2.8 Turn right at the junction with Falls Ravine Trail, next to a restroom and pavilion, and climb the hill.

3.2 At the junction with Lower Riverview Trail, turn left to walk through some young woods.

3.9 Turn right onto Riverview Trail here.

4.6 Turn right at the junction with Riverview Extension Trail, heading down the hill.

4.9 Notice on your left the park's outdoor classroom, site of many education programs.

5.1 Arrive back at the parking lot.

GREEN TIP

Go out of your way to avoid birds and animals that are mating or taking care of their young.

5 Riverview Park

Riverview Park, located just north of Pittsburgh's downtown, was once an amusement park of sorts. Today its merry-go-round is long gone. If you enjoy walking through the woods and are intrigued by the opportunity to enjoy nature and wildlife surprisingly close to the heart of one the state's biggest cities, though, this might be the hike for you.

Start: Riverview Park Visitor Center
Distance: 3.9-mile loop
Approximate hiking time: 4 hours
Difficulty: Easy to moderate
Trail surface: Dirt paths
Seasons: Year-round
Other trail users: Cross-country skiers, joggers, and horseback riders
Canine compatibility: Leashed dogs permitted
Land status: City park

Fees and permits: No fees or permits required
Maps: Map available by contacting Pittsburgh Parks and Recreation; USGS Pittsburgh West
Trail contacts: Pittsburgh Parks and Recreation, 414 Grant Street, Room 400, Pittsburgh 15219; (412) 255-2539; www.city.pittsburgh .pa.us/parks/index.html
Special considerations: There is only limited parking near the park entrance. A park map will show you where you are allowed to go.

Finding the trailhead: Take US Highway 19 (Marshall Avenue) north to a T, then turn left onto Perrysville Avenue (still US 19 north). Turn left onto Riverview Avenue to enter the park. At the entrance turn right to go to the Allegheny Observatory or left to enter the park. *DeLorme: Pennsylvania Atlas & Gazetteer:* Page 71 A5. Trailhead GPS coordinates: N40 28.970 / W80 01.093

The Hike

Look at a map of Riverview Park and you'll see an area called "the bear pit." It marks a spot that indeed held bears in the late 1800s and early 1900s.

They weren't bruins of the wild sort, however. Those disappeared years earlier when the early settlers of Pittsburgh cleared the land, wiping out predators when and where they could find them. This bear pit—in the center of what was Riverview Park in its early days, a combination zoo/amusement park/entertainment center—held captive animals.

Today there aren't any bears left, domestic or otherwise. Riverview Park remains, however, and ironically enough is home to lots of real wildlife again. White-tailed deer, squirrels, turkeys, red-tailed hawks, coyotes, rabbits, groundhogs, and a whole host of birds live in this park, which has reverted to woodlands. If there is one thing the park is missing, it's people—Riverview gets fewer human visitors than most of the other city parks.

A hiker walks past Allegheny Obsevatory in Pittsburgh's Frick Park.

This hike follows a series of trails that hug the 287-acre park's outer boundaries. Begin by taking the Wissahickon Trail near the park's visitor center. The trail loops downhill and comes to a Y; there turn right onto Archery Trail.

Archery Trail loops around a hollow and meets Myrtle Trail at 0.4 mile. Bypass Myrtle, turning right to stay on Archery.

At 0.5 mile you'll turn left onto Snowflake Trail. It follows the hillside and eventually doubles back on itself before dropping down to a parking area on Mairdale Street. Cross the parking area and Mairdale Street, turn left, and walk up the hill until you can turn right, back into the woods, onto Bridle Trail.

You'll cross a bridge at 1.0 mile, pass a low stone wall, and meet another road at 1.1 miles. Turn right, walk to the Davis Avenue bridge, and turn left back into the woods on the lower of two trails there, Violet Lane Trail.

The skyline at the entrance to Riverview Park is dominated by the Allegheny Observatory, a major astronomical research station owned by the University of Pittsburgh. Public tours are offered April through October. Call (412) 321-2400.

Violet follows a small gully, wet only after a rain, and doubles back on itself twice before reaching a spur leading to Centennial Pavilion at 1.5 miles. Turn right here onto Snyder's Point Loop Trail, which takes you into one of the prettiest, most remote sections of the park. Once home to a roadhouse owned by the Pope family, it was also previously the site of an air raid siren. Chances are good you may see deer here.

Ignore a spur to the left leading to the parking area at 1.6 miles and stay on Snyder's Point Loop Trail until you get to a junction with Deer Hollow Trail at 2.3 miles. Turn right onto Deer Hollow, which angles downhill, reaching Killbuck Road at 2.4 miles. Cross the road and reenter the woods on the opposite side on Highwood Trail.

A look out the window of the Riverview Park nature center.

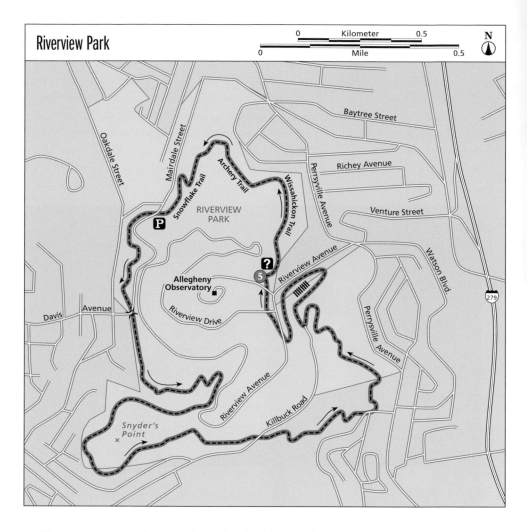

Pay attention to where you're going in this area. A somewhat confusing maze of trails, none of them marked with blazes or signs, makes it easy to take a wrong turn.

At the first T, at 2.7 miles, turn left onto Marshall Trail and walk under some telephone wires. In 100 yards or so you'll come to a four-way intersection; go straight through here. In another 100 yards the trail Ys. Turn left onto Groundhog Haven Trail, and in 0.2 mile cross a bridge and turn right.

The trail Ts again at 3.1 miles; turn left here onto Killbuck Trail. You'll cross a stream and turn left, then go left at a Y at 3.2 miles, heading downhill. The trail follows a small stream, crosses it to double back on itself, then meets with the dead end of Killbuck Road at 3.3 miles.

Turn right and walk up the road, passing a set of steps on your left at 3.4 miles. Turn left when the road Ts at 3.5 miles.

You'll pass the Old Zoo Trail on your left at 3.7 miles and an unnamed trail on your right 100 yards later. Finally Old Killbuck will bring you out to Riverview Drive. Turn right and walk back to the starting point at the park entrance.

Miles and Directions

0.0 Start at the park's visitor center, a small stone building located on the right as soon as you enter the park.

0.1 Come to a junction with Archery Trail. Turn right onto Archery Trail to stay on track.

0.5 At a junction with Snowflake Trail, turn left and ultimately downhill.

1.1 Look on your right for the Davis Avenue bridge, which is closed to vehicle traffic.

1.5 Here you'll notice a sign on the left for a spur leading to Centennial Pavilion. Bypass this as you go right.

2.4 Deer Hollow Trail crosses Killbuck Road here, then reenters the woods as Highwood Trail.

3.3 The trail meets with Killbuck Road. Turn right and follow the road.

3.4 Bypass a set of steps on the left, which you'll see as you're climbing the hill.

3.7 The trail meets the paved road again. Turn right onto Riverview Drive to close the loop.

3.9 Arrive back at the visitor center.

GREEN TIP
Keep your dog on a leash unless you are certain it can follow your voice and sight commands. Even then, keep the leash handy and your dog in sight. Do not let it approach other people and their pets unless invited to do so.

6 Youghiogheny River Trail

The Youghiogheny (Yough) River Trail is part of the Great Allegheny Passage—a 150-mile rail trail connecting Pittsburgh with Cumberland, Maryland, through a connection to the C&O Canal path that will let you go 316 miles and all the way to Washington, DC. This particular section of trail follows the path of what was a Pittsburgh & Lake Erie Railroad line and is a very popular trail with everyone from day hikers to runners.

Start: The Arthur H. King II access area in West Newton
Distance: 6.0-mile shuttle
Approximate hiking time: 2–2.5 hours
Difficulty: Easy—flat and wide
Trail surface: Crushed limestone
Seasons: Year-round
Other trail users: Bicyclists, cross-country skiers, joggers, snowshoers, and horseback riders
Canine compatibility: Leashed dogs permitted

Land status: Rail trail
Fees and permits: No fees or permits required
Maps: Map available by contacting the Regional Trail Corporation; USGS Donora
Trail contacts: Regional Trail Corporation, PO Box 95, West Newton 15089; (724) 872-5586
Special considerations: This rail trail is generally in the open, without shade, so be prepared for lots of sun.

Finding the trailhead: From Interstate 70 take exit 51B to Route 31 west to Route 136, which leads into West Newton. Cross a bridge over the Yough River and make an immediate left into the parking lot. *DeLorme: Pennsylvania Atlas & Gazetteer:* Page 71 C7. Trailhead GPS coordinates: N40 12.668 / W79 46.214

The Hike

Mine disasters often make national headlines. Think of the Sago Mine in West Virginia in 2006, where twelve men lost their lives. Television and the Internet were broadcasting news of that event even as the families of the miners were still crying fresh tears over the loss of fathers, sons, and husbands.

That's not new. Neither, unfortunately, is the grim reality of mine disasters.

Consider the case of the Port Royal No. 2 mine disaster, which took place in West Newton on June 10, 1901. The far-off *New York Times* described the accident this way just one day after the event: "Not a practical miner in this district believes that one of the sixteen men entombed in the Port Royal Mine by the explosion last night is still alive. There is no fire in the mine, to judge from appearances at the pit mouth, but the force of the explosion was so great that none of the men, so the miners say, could have survived the shock."

Ultimately at least twenty, perhaps thirty, miners and would-be rescuers died in the incident.

The entrance to West Newton Cemetery, as seen from the Yough River Trail.

Today a monument to those lost souls exists along the Youghiogheny River Trail, a rail trail that parallels the "Yough," as the river is known locally, and covers 43.0 miles in its northern section. It's just one of several interesting sights along this hike, which covers 6.0 miles on a shuttle hike and 12.0 miles on an out-and-back walk.

Pick up the trail at the Arthur H. King II access in West Newton and turn right (upstream) to head south along the trail. This walk is perfectly flat on a bed of crushed stone, so it's very easy.

You'll pass the first of several benches at the 0.5-mile mark. Go around a gate at 0.7 mile; there's a monument explaining the history of Buddtown on your left.

The trail passes beneath a power line at 1.0 mile and over a road, with posted property along each side of the trail, at 1.5 miles. Deer tracks in the wet edges show that it's not just people that use this trail. Fox squirrels are common, too.

Just beyond this area, the hillside rises almost vertically from the trail on your right. Water trickles over these bluffs in numerous places, creating mini-waterfalls in summer and daggerlike stalactites of opaque ice in winter.

Mile 3.1 brings you to perhaps the most beautiful section of the trail. A bridge here at the Cedar Creek Gorge—and a side trail worthy of exploration, particularly in spring when the wildflowers are in bloom—showcases this stream as it flows to the river.

A hiker, seen in the distance, walks from West Newton toward Cedar Creek.

Another 0.2 mile brings you to Cedar Creek Station in Cedar Creek County Park. The station itself, which sells refreshments and rents bicycles, is open from April to October. Year-round, though, you can use a restroom, launch a boat, or picnic at one of the many tables. There's even a lean-to for campers and bigger open spaces for Scout groups to pitch tents. All that makes this is a nice ending spot in its own right if you want to shorten this hike a bit.

Otherwise, continue on until, at 4.6 miles, you come to Saw Mill Run and the marker for the Port Royal Mine disaster. The I-70 bridge at 5.6 miles is the next landmark. Continue following the trail to the parking area in Smithton at 6.0 miles, where your shuttle awaits.

Miles and Directions

0.0 Park and begin your hike at the Arthur H. King II access area.

0.5 A small bench offers a relaxing spot to sit and view the Yough River.

0.7 Look on your left near the gate for the Buddtown historical marker, which offers a glimpse into the town that used to be here.

1.5 Come to a road crossing and a small industrial site. Continue straight along the trail.

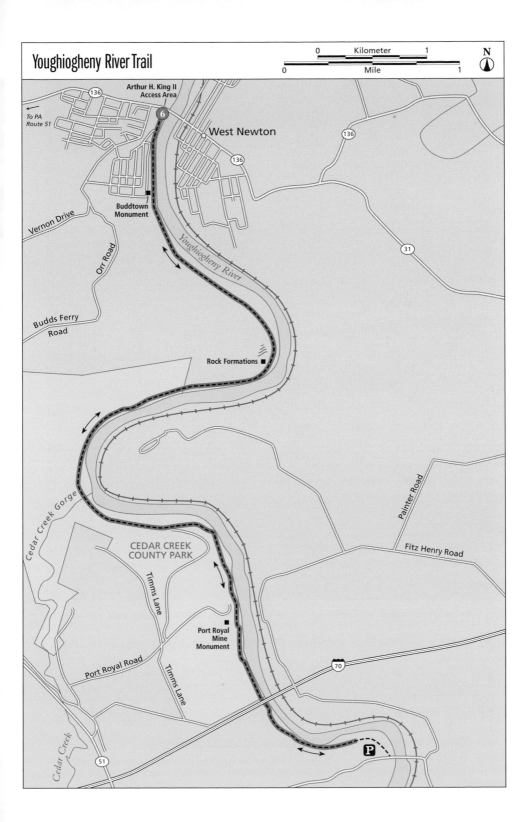

Youghiogheny River Trail

0 — Kilometer — 1

0 — Mile — 1

N

To PA
Route 51

136

Arthur H. King II
Access Area

6

West Newton

136

136

31

Buddtown
Monument

Vernon Drive

Orr Road

Youghiogheny River

Budds Ferry
Road

Rock Formations

Cedar Creek Gorge

CEDAR CREEK
COUNTY PARK

Timms Lane

Port Royal Road

Timms Lane

Port Royal
Mine
Monument

Painter Road

Fitz Henry Road

70

51

Cedar Creek

P

Fall leaves on the Yough River Trail.

3.1 A bridge over Cedar Creek and a trail to the right announce that you're in the Cedar Creek Gorge.

3.3 Cedar Creek Station is a spot where you can buy some refreshments (in summer) or picnic at a table.

4.6 Look on your right for the Port Royal Mine disaster historical marker, which details the tragedy that captivated a nation.

5.6 Cross under the tall I-70 bridge, which carries truck traffic over the river.

6.0 Reach the Smithton access area, which has its own parking lot and picnic pavilion, and pick up your shuttle vehicle.

7 Slippery Rock Gorge

Part of the North Country National Scenic Trail, this is without a doubt one of the most challenging hikes you can do. Though just more than 6.0 miles long, it is very steep, particularly in the northeastern end of McConnells Mill State Park, near Eckert Bridge. It's worth visiting, though. Slippery Rock Gorge is a place of dramatic scenery—but you'll want to do this as a shuttle hike.

Start: Breakneck Bridge (**Option:** Hell's Hollow parking area for reverse hike)
Distance: 6.2-mile shuttle
Approximate hiking time: 4.5–5 hours
Difficulty: Difficult, with a number of steep climbs up narrow trails
Trail surface: Dirt paths
Seasons: Year-round; best hiked May to October
Other trail users: None
Canine compatibility: Leashed dogs permitted
Land status: State park
Fees and permits: No fees or permits required

Maps: Map available by contacting McConnells Mill State Park; USGS Portersville
Trail contacts: McConnells Mill State Park, RR 2 Box 16, Portersville 16051-9401; (724) 368-8091; www.dcnr.state.pa.us/stateparks/parks/mcconnellsmill.aspx
Special considerations: This area can be very pretty when there's snow on the ground, but it can also be very difficult and even dangerous to hike in winter. If you're thinking of hiking when there may be ice, call the park first for an update on the advisability of walking here.

Finding the trailhead: Follow Interstate 79 north to Route 488 west. Turn north onto US Highway 19 in Portersville, then left onto Cheeseman Road and the parking area for Eckert and Breakneck Bridges. *DeLorme: Pennsylvania Atlas & Gazetteer:* Page 57 A4. Trailhead GPS coordinates: N40 56.244 / W80 10.707

The Hike

Slippery Rock Gorge is as magnificent a site as you will see anywhere. Deep, with Slippery Rock Creek pouring over giant boulders, fast enough to qualify as whitewater, it's a place of awe-inspiring scenery. Hiking it, though, is equally extreme.

You'll have to make several steep climbs—you climb and drop, climb and drop more than once—on trails that can be narrow, so caution is in order here. This shouldn't be your first hike, either. Tackle this one only after you've worked yourself into shape elsewhere.

You can make things a little easier on yourself by starting this hike near Eckert Bridge. That gets the toughest walking out of the way first, while you're still fresh.

The trail first passes through a rocky area that runs close to the creek. The blue-blazed trail is easy to follow, but there's typically some poison ivy here, so watch for that. On the far side of the creek, you'll see where a feeder stream, Cheeseman Run, enters the gorge. There's a popular rock climbing area by Breakneck Bridge.

The trail through Slippery Rock Gorge is rocky and rough, with lots of roots clinging to thin soil along the creek edge.

Continue along, making several of the climbs mentioned earlier, until the first of the really serious ascents begins at 0.6 mile. This climb isn't long, roughly 0.1 mile, but it will get your attention. You'll pass through hemlocks, which you'll likely get to admire when you stop to catch your breath.

Pass through a mature hardwood forest, crossing several seeps, and you'll find yourself on a bench with some interesting cliffs on your right at 1.1 miles.

Now it's time to go downhill again. The trail twists and turns as it switchbacks its way downslope. Finally, at 2.1 miles, you'll emerge into an area known as Walnut Flats. This is flat country, so you'll get a chance to relax a bit.

You'll be entering the widest part of this narrow state park. That means it's also the most remote. The Slippery Rock Gorge Trail is the only way in or out, so no one gets here unless they really mean to. That offers you the chance to enjoy some solitude, all at creek level.

The trail follows a bench, dropping down into occasional ravines. There's some old-growth forest here, including oaks and hemlocks.

Mile 3.8 brings you to a Y in the trail. Turning left onto an unblazed trail leads to the spot where Hell Run feeds into Slippery Rock Creek. There is a small waterfall there, but the park recommends that you view it only by staying on the established trail. Veer right to follow the blue blazes.

◀ *A look downstream along Slippery Rock Creek in McConnells Mill State Park, which is home to Slippery Rock Gorge.*

Slippery Rock Gorge

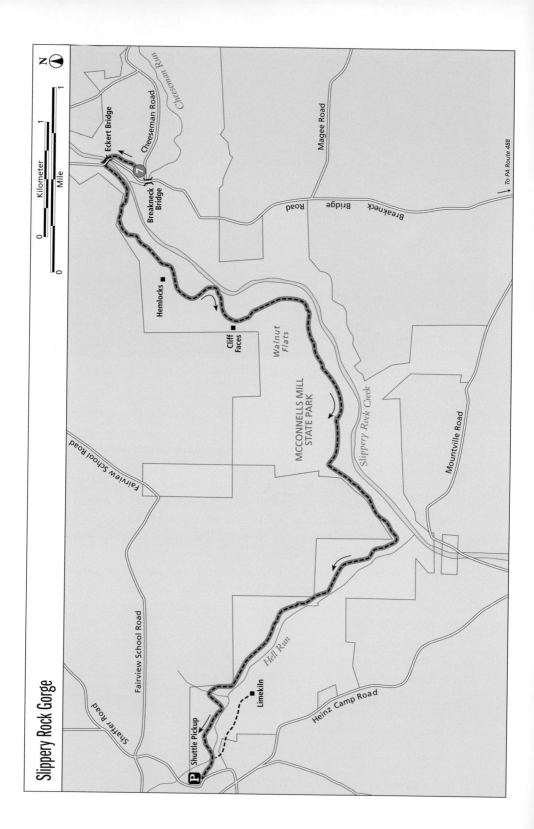

N

Kilometer
0   1

Mile
0   1

Eckert Bridge

Cheeseman Road

Cheeseman Run

Breakneck Bridge

Breakneck Bridge Road

To PA Route 488

Magee Road

Hemlocks

Cliff Faces

Walnut Flats

Fairview School Road

MCCONNELLS MILL STATE PARK

Slippery Rock Creek

Mountville Road

Shaffer Road

Fairview School Road

Hell Run

Shuttle Pickup

Limekiln

Heinz Camp Road

P

While you're here, it's worth checking out the covered bridge and old mill on Slippery Rock Creek, farther upstream along Kennedy Road. The bridge was built in 1874 and is one of just two covered bridges in Lawrence County. The mill is even older. The first gristmill on this site was constructed in 1852. It burnt down but was rebuilt in 1868 and renovated in 1875. One of the first rolling mills in the country, it closed for good in 1928 because of sagging profits.

You'll cross an unnamed side stream and begin to climb again. Mile 5.2 brings you very close to the park boundary; white blazes on your right mark the start of some private property.

Descend again, crossing a bridge at 5.5 miles. Mile 5.9 brings you to a Y in the trail; to the left is Hell's Hollow Trail. It leads to an old limekiln and a waterfall, if you're inclined to take another side trip.

Otherwise, turn right and walk to the Hell's Hollow parking lot, where you'll pick up your shuttle vehicle.

Miles and Directions

0.0 Start at the Eckert Bridge parking area.

0.6 Begin the first steep climb of the hike.

1.1 Look here for some interesting rock cliffs on your right.

2.1 Walnut Flats represents the easiest part of the hike, as well as the most remote.

3.8 The junction of Hell Run and Slippery Rock Creeks here is also site of an unblazed trail to the left. Instead, turn right.

5.5 Cross a footbridge here after descending on the trail.

5.9 At the junction with Hell's Hollow Trail, turn right and cross a small footbridge.

6.2 Finish at the Hell's Hollow parking area, where you'll pick up your shuttle vehicle.

GREEN TIP

Carry a reusable water container that you fill at the tap. Bottled water is expensive, lots of petroleum is used to make the plastic bottles, and they're a disposal nightmare.

8 Beechwood Farms Nature Reserve

A relatively short hike through a nature preserve that contains just 134 acres, this loop is nonetheless enjoyable, especially if you want to stay close to Pittsburgh. Beechwood is owned by the Audubon Society of Western Pennsylvania, so you can expect to see lots of birds here, especially at the feeders behind the nature center. There are opportunities to see a variety of flora and fauna as well. You can lengthen any visit here by coordinating it with one of Beechwood's many programs or a trip to its nature store.

Start: Beechwood Farms Nature Center
Distance: 2.8-mile loop
Approximate hiking time: 1–2 hours
Difficulty: Easy to moderate, with just a few short hills
Trail surface: Dirt paths and lawn surfaces. Spring Hollow Trail is maintained as an "all peoples" trail, meaning that while it's not ADA compliant, it has been constructed to adhere to as many of those principles as possible, given the topography. It gets mulched every third year and averages 6 feet wide.
Seasons: Year-round
Other trail users: Cross-country skiers
Canine compatibility: Dogs prohibited unless they are special-needs animals

Land status: Owned by the Western Pennsylvania Conservancy and leased to Audubon Society of Western Pennsylvania
Fees and permits: No fees or permits required
Maps: Map available by contacting the Audubon Society of Western Pennsylvania; USGS Glenshaw
Trail contacts: Audubon Society of Western Pennsylvania, 614 Dorseyville Road, Pittsburgh 15238; (412) 963-6100; www.aswp.org
Special considerations: Individual trails here are closed periodically in winter for the purposes of managing deer. While most of the reserve's trails are not blazed, they are marked at each intersection, so getting around is pretty simple.

Finding the trailhead: From exit 48 of the Pennsylvania Turnpike, get onto Route 910/Yellow Belt. Turn left onto Locust Hill Road and go 1.4 miles. Turn right onto Guys Run Road and then right onto the Green Belt. After traveling 1.3 miles, turn left onto Dorseyville Road and follow it to the nature reserve. *DeLorme: Pennsylvania Atlas & Gazetteer:* Page 57 D6. Trailhead GPS coordinates: N40 32.574 / W79 54.355

The Hike

It's hard to imagine finding a working dairy farm in Fox Chapel these days. The community is one of the most affluent suburbs of Pittsburgh, with estates owned by some of the most prominent families in the area.

It's possible to take a little bit of Beechwood home with you. The Audubon Society has a native plant center where you can buy species common to Allegheny County and western Pennsylvania for landscaping. Call (412) 963-6100 or visit www.aswp.org.

A tufted titmouse at a feeder outside the visitor center at Beechwood Farms Nature Reserve.

Yet a century ago, Beechwood Farms was indeed an actual farm. Owner William Flinn didn't necessarily have to take his living from the land. He had retired to the life of a gentleman farmer only after a long and successful career in politics, which ended with his being a state senator. The farm wasn't just a country estate either, though. Flinn raised a whole host of domestic animals on site, most notably Guernsey cattle, and supplied his Pittsburgh neighbors with fresh dairy products.

Today 134 acres of what remains of the farm have been set aside for the benefit of nature and those who enjoy it as Beechwood Farms Nature Reserve. Owned by

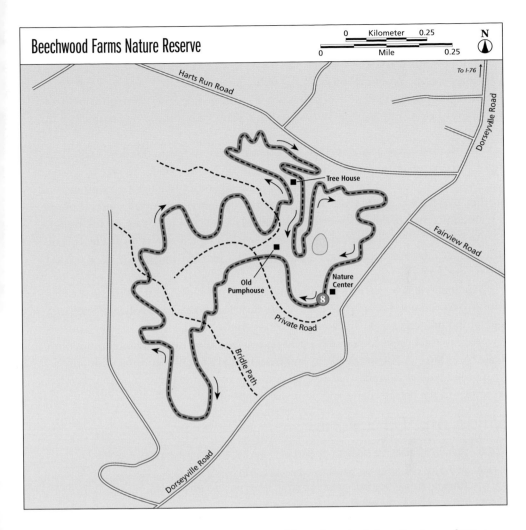

0   Kilometer   0.25

0   Mile   0.25

N

Harts Run Road

To I-76

Dorseyville Road

Tree House

Fairview Road

Old Pumphouse

Nature Center

8

Private Road

Bridle Path

Dorseyville Road

the Western Pennsylvania Conservancy and leased to Audubon Society of Western Pennsylvania, it offers 5.0 miles of hiking trails, organized opportunities to study nature, a store, and more.

To start this hike, which covers 2.8 miles and winds through the most far-flung portions of the reserve, follow the sidewalk between the nature store and education building. Turn left and head uphill on Spring Hollow Trail.

At 0.2 mile turn left, cross a private road, and follow Meadow View Trail. Cover another 0.1 mile, then turn left onto Pine Hollow Trail. This is one of the longest individual trails in the reserve and a walk that often involves deer sightings.

◀ *Top: Benches located outside the Beechwood Farms Nature Reserve visitor center offer the chance to sit and enjoy nature.*
Bottom: A weather vane atop the Beechwood Farms Nature Reserve visitor center.

Cross a bridge at 0.5 mile and then another at a pretty waterfall at 0.8 mile. At 1.1 miles ignore a trail leading to the left that's blocked with brush; continue straight on Pine Hollow. You'll take the next left just a 100 feet or so farther on.

Come to an old pumphouse at 1.2 miles. Turn left onto Meadow View here. Recross the private road at 1.4 miles; you'll walk a short way through a field of goldenrod before turning left onto Woodland Trail, where the forest is thick with grapevines.

At 1.6 miles cross a small bridge and turn right onto Spring Hollow Trail. Turn right at the next junction with Violet Trail, too (you'll come back this way later).

You'll pass a few benches, but if you want a really neat place to stop, continue on to the "tree house" at 1.8 miles. Really a platform that you can walk onto, it offers a panoramic view of the valley below, particularly when the leaves are off the trees.

At 1.85 miles you'll leave Spring Hollow by turning left onto Upper Fields Trail. Turn left at the next junction, at 2.1 miles, onto Goldenrod Trail. You're back behind the nature center here.

The trail will take you by a pond where you can see birds and frogs in the warmer months. At the pond's edge you'll see a signpost for Violet Trail. Follow Violet to a sign at 2.2 miles that says "To Woodland." Turn right here.

Walk to the bridge you crossed earlier, turn right, then turn left at 2.3 miles onto Oak Forest Trail. A few of the plants and trees in this area are identified with signs.

Cross a road at 2.4 miles, heading toward the pond. At the next junction turn left to return to the nature center and your starting point.

Miles and Directions

0.0 Start by following the sidewalk as it leads to the left and around the nature center.

0.2 At the top of a small hill, turn left at the junction of Spring Hollow and Meadow View Trails. (**Option:** A short side trip, marked by signs, takes you to a small vista.)

0.5 Cross an open, and sometimes muddy, bridle trail.

0.8 Cross a small bridge that sits at the head of a waterfall.

1.2 Bypass the old pumphouse, which still has a few pieces of rusted machinery within its rickety walls.

1.8 Come to a walkway leading to the "Treetop" tree house, an elevated platform that affords a nice view of the woods below, especially in winter when the leaves are off the trees.

2.1 Pass the pond study area, which is frequented by Canada geese and other birds.

2.8 Return to the nature center, noting the feeders here that are always busy with cardinals, woodpeckers, and other birds.

GREEN TIP
Pass it down—the best way to instill good green habits in your children is to set a good example.

9 Glacier Ridge Trail

Part of the larger North Country National Scenic Trail, the Glacier Ridge Trail extends 14.0 miles across Moraine State Park. Within Moraine, the trail travels through pine plantations, mature and regenerating forests, and past a pond; offers views of the expansive Lake Arthur; and provides plenty of opportunities to view wildlife. This particular hike is an out-and-back walk, with a small loop at one end.

Start: The Glacier Ridge trailhead on North Shore Drive
Distance: 8.2-mile lollipop
Approximate hiking time: 3.5–4.5 hours
Difficulty: Moderate to difficult, with some steep hills and narrow trails
Trail surface: Dirt paths
Seasons: Year-round
Other trail users: Hunters
Canine compatibility: Leashed dogs permitted

Land status: State park
Fees and permits: No fees or permits required
Maps: Map available by contacting Moraine State Park; USGS Prospect
Trail contacts: Moraine State Park, 225 Pleasant Valley Road, Portersville 16051-9650; (724) 368-8811; www.dcnr.state.pa.us/state parks/parks/moraine.aspx
Special considerations: This area is open to hunting, so wear orange during hunting season.

Finding the trailhead: Take US Highway 422 west from Prospect, then turn right onto the North Shore ramp. Follow North Shore Drive to the Glacier Ridge trailhead. *DeLorme: Pennsylvania Atlas & Gazetteer:* Page 57 A5. Trailhead GPS coordinates: N40 58.486 / W80 07.342

The Hike

A short drive north on Interstate 79, Moraine State Park is a popular destination for Pittsburghers. They come here in big numbers to fish, swim, picnic, and hike. Few likely think of it as wilderness of any kind.

Yet Moraine is home to a surprising variety of wildlife. It's got the usual deer, squirrels, turkeys, and songbirds. Foxes and raccoons are common, too. And don't be surprised if you see a coyote.

Spread all across Pennsylvania these days, coyotes do very well here. Scats full of fruits and berries and—especially after deer season—chunks of hair and hide can be seen right on the trail if you keep your eyes open.

To begin this hike, park at the trailhead on North Shore Drive, at the western end of Lake Arthur near the McDanel's Launch Area. The trail is blazed blue and easy to follow. It's flat at the beginning but boggy, too, so be prepared for potentially wet feet.

The trail enters the woods at 0.3 mile and crosses a service road at 0.4 mile. It then meanders through woods alternately thick with grapevines and greenbriers sprouting up among some oaks.

The Glacier Ridge trailhead in Moraine State Park.

You'll cross a bridge over a small creek at 1.4 miles. Mile 1.5 brings you to an intersection that leads to a shelter. Turn left and travel uphill through a stand of pines, following the blue blazes. Deer tracks are often abundant here.

Turn left at a Y in the trail at 1.6 miles and then left again at a T in the trail near a water tower at 1.7 miles. In another 0.5 mile you'll pass near the park boundary, with some posted private ground on your left. The trail then follows the edge of a hollow at 2.5 miles. This area is popular with deer hunters, so make sure you're wearing orange during hunting season, especially if you are here in early December.

Pass a giant water tower, emblazoned with graffiti, just before crossing Mt. Union Road at 3.0 miles. Cross the road and follow the trail as its circles a pond. This waterway seems to be perpetually overflowing in spring and fall, so expect to do some fancy stepping if you want to get around it and still keep your feet dry.

Another Y in the trail crops up at 3.2 miles. Turn right here, leaving the Glacier Ridge Trail, to head toward the Davis Hollow Marina. Fox and coyote sign is often evident here amidst the multitude of grapevines. Look for lots of gray squirrels, too.

Mile 3.7 brings you to another Y in the trail. To go right is to head for the marina. Instead, turn left and follow the blue blazes. In another 0.2 mile you'll pass the Davis Hollow Outdoor Center on your right. There's often a lot of bird activity here.

Follow the trail up the hollow to a Y at 4.1 miles. Turn left and follow the yellow and blue blazes along a section of trail that's rocky and often wet. This is again the Glacier Ridge Trail.

A view of Lake Arthur in Moraine State Park, just off Glacier Ridge Trail.

You'll be walking up a small grade when, at 4.6 miles, the trail makes a sharp left. Keep an eye out for this—the trail also seems to go straight here, but if you go that way, you'll run out of blazes.

Mile 5.0 brings you to the Y where you turned to go toward the marina. This time turn right, circle the pond again, and follow Glacier Ridge back to the starting point.

THE EASTERN COYOTE

Perhaps no other animal is as misunderstood as the eastern coyote.

Coyotes have been in Pennsylvania since the 1940s, but their numbers really took off between the 1970s and 1990s. Today they can be found in each of the state's sixty-seven counties. The state's second-biggest predator, coyotes commonly weigh thirty to fifty pounds. Some get larger still, making them twice as big as their counterparts in the western United States.

Coyotes are smart, adaptable predators that eat anything and everything from squirrels and house pets to berries and garden vegetables. Though some believed they were released into Pennsylvania by wildlife officials, the truth is that they've simply taken advantage of abundant food sources to expand their range all across the northeastern United States.

Glacier Ridge Trail

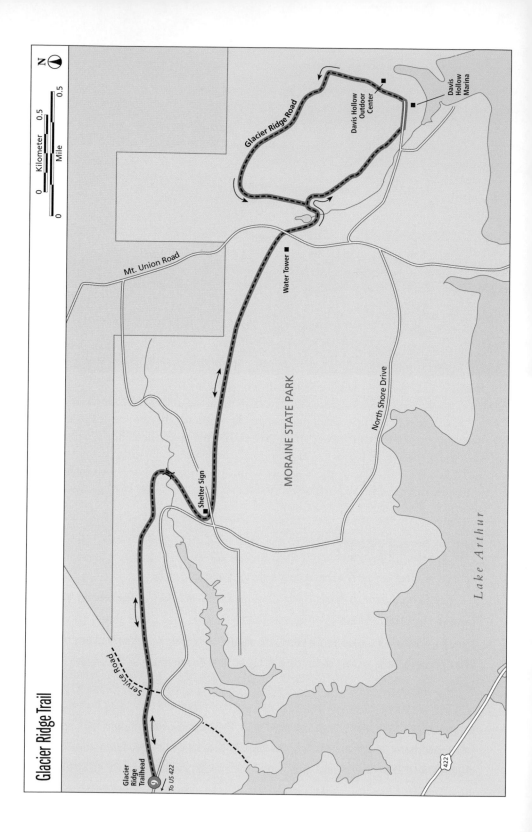

N

0   0.5   Kilometer
0   0.5   Mile

Glacier Ridge Road

Davis Hollow Outdoor Center

Davis Hollow Marina

Mt. Union Road

Water Tower

MORAINE STATE PARK

North Shore Drive

Shelter Sign

Service Road

Glacier Ridge Trailhead

To US 422

Lake Arthur

422

Miles and Directions

0.0 Start at the roadside parking area for the trailhead near McDanel's Launch.

0.4 Cross a wide but grassy service road to stay on the trail.

1.4 Cross a bridge in a stream bottom, being sure to look for animal tracks in the bank.

1.7 Come to a junction near a big water tower on your right. Turn left and start uphill through the woods.

3.0 Bypass another water tower, this one covered in graffiti, and Cross Mt. Union Road.

3.1 You'll see a small pond here. Circle it, keeping it on your left.

3.2 At a Y in the trail, turn right and head toward the marina.

3.7 At another Y, turn left and follow the blue blazes.

3.9 Look to your right and you'll see the Davis Hollow Outdoor Center, which hosts a number of education programs.

4.1 Climb a short ways, keeping the outdoor center at your back, and then turn left at a Y in the trail.

5.0 You're back at the junction with the marina trail. This time turn right and head back toward the pond as you retrace your steps to your vehicle.

8.2 Arrive back at your starting point.

GREEN TIP
Keep to established trails as much as possible.
If there aren't any, stay on surfaces that will be least affected, like rock, gravel, dry grasses, or snow.

10 Jennings Environmental Education Center

At 3.0 miles, this is one of the shortest hikes in the book. It's a relatively easy one, too, with just one challenging climb. But that doesn't mean you can't make a day out of visiting Jennings Environmental Education Center. The center routinely hosts programs for children and adults on everything from tree identification and wildflowers to rattlesnakes and Native American culture. Most are free, and all are open to the public, so you can often plan a hike around another opportunity to learn about nature.

Start: The visitor parking lot near the entrance to the park's prairie
Distance: 3.0-mile loop
Approximate hiking time: 2 hours
Difficulty: Easy to moderate, with flat terrain
Trail surface: Dirt paths
Seasons: Year round; especially good in late July or early August, when the park's prairie is in full bloom
Other trail users: Cross-country skiers and snowshoers
Canine compatibility: Leashed dogs permitted
Land status: State park
Fees and permits: No fees or permits required

Schedule: Check with the park for a calendar of events and a program schedule.
Maps: Map available by contacting the Jennings Environmental Education Center; USGS Slippery Rock
Trail contacts: Jennings Environmental Education Center, 2951 Prospect Road, Slippery Rock 16057-8701; (724) 794-6011; www .dcnr.state.pa.us/stateparks/parks/jennings .aspx
Special considerations: If you walk your dog through Jennings's prairie—which is also home to endangered massasauga rattlesnakes—be sure to keep your pet on a leash so that neither he nor the snakes get hurt.

Finding the trailhead: Jennings Environmental Education Center is located near Slippery Rock, just off Route 8 about 12.5 miles north of Butler. *DeLorme: Pennsylvania Atlas & Gazetteer:* Page 43 D5. Trailhead GPS coordinates: N41 00.593 / W80 00.287

The Hike

The eastern massasauga is an unusual creature by Pennsylvania standards, so it's only fitting that it survives best in a place that's equally unique.

The massasauga is a rattlesnake, one of three kinds that live in Pennsylvania. It's the smallest—20 to 30 inches—and by far the most rare. Found only in the western third of the state, they need old fields and meadows marked by low-lying wet spots with higher dry ground nearby. That mix is increasingly hard to find, and the snakes have suffered as a result, so much so that they're on the state's endangered species list.

There's always something in bloom at Jennings Environmental Education Center.

One place where they're doing relatively well is Jennings Environmental Education Center, a state park property north of Butler. That's because Jennings contains twenty acres of prairie habitat reminiscent of what you would see in the Midwest.

On this hike you can check out the only publicly owned relict prairie in the state, perhaps see a massasauga rattlesnake, and assuredly see a colorful quilt of blazing star and other wildflowers.

To begin, park in the lot adjacent to the prairie. Follow the path and, in less than 200 feet, you'll see a sign for the Blazing Star Trail. Continue straight ahead, being sure to notice the shingle oak.

At 0.1 mile turn right onto the Prairie Loop Trail. It's not necessarily quiet here—the trail runs adjacent to Route 173, so you'll hear traffic. But this area also provides the best glimpse at the prairie, so it's worth it. Interpretive signs explain what to look for.

Mile 0.4 brings you to another junction. Turn right onto Blazing Star Trail, then make another right onto Deer Trail, which winds through a regenerating woodlot.

Turn right onto Oak Woods Trail at 0.6 mile. Cross a bridge at 1.1 miles, climb a short hill, and at 1.4 miles head downhill past a bench to a low, wet area marked by a multitude of stumps. At 1.5 miles turn right and cross a bridge onto Hepatica Trail.

A sign in Jennings Environmental Education Center's prairie, explaining the soils under your feet.

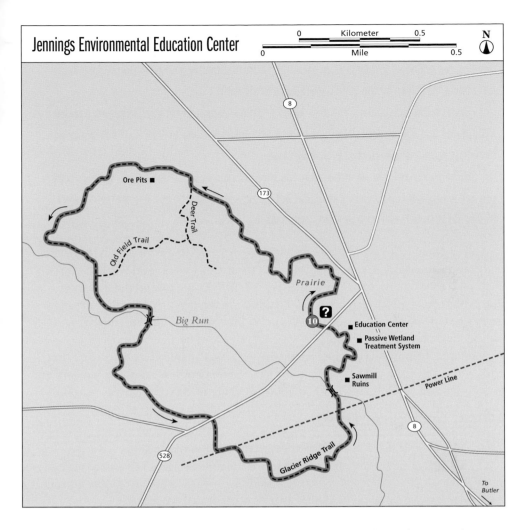

Kilometer
0   0.5
Mile
0   0.5

N

Ore Pits ■

Deer Trail

Old Field Trail

173

8

Prairie

?

10

Big Run

Education Center ■

Passive Wetland
Treatment System ■

Sawmill
Ruins ■

Power Line

528

8

Glacier Ridge Trail

To
Butler

After climbing out of this lowland, you'll come to a Y in the trail at 1.7 miles. Turn right onto Glacier Ridge Trail, which crosses Route 528 and enters Moraine State Park for a short while. Ignore the black blazes here, meant to blot out marks made by mistake, as you trek uphill steeply enough to get your chest thumping.

The trail crosses a power line at 1.8 miles and splits. Turn left onto the blue-blazed North Country Trail and then turn right at 1.85 miles, up the hill, onto Ridge Trail.

Continue on Ridge, ignoring the trail on the right that goes to a private campground, and wind your way back to the power line. At 2.2 miles turn left onto Black Cherry Trail. Stay on Black Cherry, past bridges on the left at 2.3 and 2.5 miles, until you're ultimately following a small stream tinted orange by acid mine drainage.

At 2.6 miles turn left and cross a bridge onto Old Mill Trail. This will take you past the ruins of an old sawmill and to a series of ponds that serve as a passive treatment system, which is helping eliminate the mine drainage problem.

"IMPROVING" THE PRAIRIE

Keeping the prairie at Jennings Environmental Education Center a prairie—that is, keeping it from being overtaken by the forest—requires a little work.

Each year in mid-January, the park hosts a "prairie improvement day." Volunteers armed with gloves and sturdy shoes turn out to do a little housecleaning of sorts. It's also a good chance to learn more about the prairie up close.

There's a reward, too. Volunteers are fed soup donated by local restaurants in mugs that you get to take home. Everyone's welcome, but participants must be at least twelve years old. Preregistration is required; call (724) 794-6011.

Circle around the ponds counterclockwise so that you wind up at a shelter with informational signs explaining how the treatment system works. When you've checked that out, jump onto Wood Whisperer Trail, heading toward the park education center. At 2.7 miles turn left when the trail Ts and follow it along an observation deck. Feeders here make this a good spot to photograph birds like doves, black-capped chickadees, and cardinals.

Continue behind the building until you see a sign pointing to the prairie-area trails where you parked. There are a few picnic tables here, making this a nice place to rest up or eat lunch before heading home or taking in one of the park's programs.

Miles and Directions

0.0 Start at the parking lot at the trailhead leading to the park's prairie area.

0.1 Bear right at the junction with the Prairie Loop Trail to circle the prairie, keeping it on your left.

0.6 Having circled the prairie, turn right to enter the woods along Oak Woods Trail.

1.1 Find a couple of stumps cut to serve as chairs, complete with backs, that make a nice resting spot.

1.7 At the junction with the Glacier Ridge Trail, turn right and cross Route 528 to follow the path that leads to Moraine State Park.

1.8 Cross under a power line, which is a good place to spot deer.

2.6 Bypass an old sawmill ruins. Note the cut stone that once marked what must have been an impressive building.

2.7 A mini-shelter, complete with benches and signs, explains the passive acid mine drainage treatment system in place here. Turn left at the T in the trail.

3.0 Having walked past the park's nature center, finish the hike back at the parking area.

Honorable Mentions

A. Keystone State Park

At just 1,200 acres, a relatively small park by state standards, Keystone State Park nonetheless offers opportunities to hike. Located just off US Highway 22 in Westmoreland County, the park is easy to get to. Its 6.0 miles of trails—which offer mostly easy walking—include the 2.5-mile Davis Run Trail. For information call (724) 668-2939 or visit www.dcnr.state.pa.us/stateparks/parks/keystone.aspx.

B. McConnells Mill State Park

Site of the previously described Slippery Rock Gorge Trail, McConnells Mill is also home to two other trails worth mentioning. The 2.0-mile Kildoo Trail and 1.5-mile Alpha Pass Trail offer milder, though not necessarily easy, hiking. Alpha Pass ends up at a waterfall, too. For information call (724) 368-8091 or visit www.dcnr.state.pa.us/stateparks/parks/mcconnellsmill.aspx.

C. Bushy Run Battlefield

In August 1763 British Col. Henry Bouquet was on his way to Pittsburgh—then known as Fort Pitt for the frontier stockade there—when he encountered a band of hostile Indians. The resulting two-day battle, which the British won, took place here. Today visitors can hike the battlefield's trails and visit a small museum. For information call (724) 527-5584 or visit www.bushyrunbattlefield.com.

D. Todd Sanctuary

Located about thirty minutes north of Pittsburgh in Sarver, Todd Sanctuary was the first sanctuary owned by the Audubon Society of Western Pennsylvania. It doesn't get quite as much attention as the society's other property, Beechwood Farms, but it has some nice hiking trails. You can explore them on your own or come here for the guided nature walks. For information call (412) 963-6100 or visit www.aswp.org.

E. Twin Lakes Park

Twin Lakes, located just off US Highway 30 east of Greensburg, is Westmoreland County's showcase park. It's the most highly developed, with plenty of opportunities for picnicking, fishing, and boating, but there is some hiking to be had here, too. The main walk is the loop that goes around the park's Upper and Lower Lakes. It is a little less than 2.5 miles. For information call (724) 830-3950 or visit www.co .westmoreland.pa.us/parks.

F. Rachel Carson Trail

The Rachel Carson Trail stretches 35.7 miles across northern Allegheny County, from Harrison Hills Park to North Park. It crosses county parks, follows gas and power lines, and skirts suburban homes and farms. The trail is tough in sections, partly because of terrain and partly because of encroaching development. But there are opportunities to make multiple shuttle hikes, and spurs lead to places like the Rachel Carson Homestead. For information call the Rachel Carson Trails Conservancy at (412) 366-3339 or visit www.rachelcarsontrails.org.

G. Baker Trail

One of eighteen long-distance backpacking trails in Pennsylvania, the Baker Trail stretches 141.0 miles, starting near Freeport. Trail groups, including the Rachel Carson Trails Conservancy, are working hard to get it back into shape, but it is still rough in a few places due to lack of maintenance. Be prepared to climb over blowdowns and search for faded blazes. The trail follows forest paths and paved and dirt roads. For information call the Rachel Carson Trails Conservancy at (412) 366-3339 or visit www.rachelcarsontrails.org.

H. Boyce Park

The first of Allegheny County's parks to be dedicated, and named for the founder of the Boy Scouts, Boyce Park is home to a wave pool, archery range, ski area, tennis courts, and ball fields. Maintenance of its trails—in the form of signs—has not always gotten equal priority. But if you're willing to follow some unmarked paths, you can wind through a variety of habitats and past a number of the park's other attractions. For information call (724) 327-0338 or visit www.alleghenycounty.us/parks/bpfac.aspx.

I. North Park

This is the busiest of Allegheny County's parks. With its golf course, fishing and boating lake, ice-skating rink, tennis and basketball courts, and other attractions, it is always full of people, especially on weekends. Don't come expecting solitude. It does, though, have its positives, not the least of which are its proximity to downtown and its wildlife, like deer and turkeys. Some of the trails here follow roads; others wander through woods and across fields. For information call (724) 935-1766 or visit www.alleghenycounty.us/parks/npfac.aspx.

J. Brush Creek Park

A reclaimed strip mine area, Brush Creek is located in the northeastern corner of Beaver County. It's home to 3.5 miles of trails limited to foot traffic only, but there are also some bridle trails here that you can walk. Combining the East and West Trails in a loop will give you about a 5.0-mile hike leading past some rock outcrops, a model airfield, and a springhouse. For information call (724) 846-5600 or visit www.co.beaver.pa.us/recreation/parks.htm.

K. Bradys Run Park

Sitting just off Route 51, 2 miles north of Beaver, Bradys Run Park holds one of the largest horseshoe courts in Pennsylvania. It also gets attention from anglers. But hikers can make use of this park, too. It's got more than 15.0 miles of trails, which can be linked with short hops across roads and connector paths to create some longer walks. For information call (724) 846-5600 or visit www.co.beaver.pa.us/recreation/parks.htm.

L. Point State Park

Located at the "Point" in Pittsburgh where the Allegheny and Monongahela Rivers join to form the Ohio River, this is not a big park. But if you want to know about the history of the city from its earliest days and get a look at its skyline and famous fountain, this is the place to do it. Heavy on informational signs and plaques, the 1.0-mile walk will fill you in on who's who in the city and how it came to be. You can also visit the newly renovated Fort Pitt Museum and the Fort Pitt Blockhouse, the oldest authentic building in western Pennsylvania. For information call (412) 471-0235 or visit www.dcnr.state.pa.us/stateparks/parks/point.aspx.

M. Eliza Furnace Trail

Forget birds, wildflowers, and mountain streams. This trail—also known as the "jail trail" because it passes the county lock-up—has none of those, unless you come across a stray pigeon. This is an urban trail all the way, leading from Oakland toward downtown Pittsburgh. It's as urban as urban gets, running alongside one of the major routes into the city. If you want to see some of Pittsburgh's unique bridges and landmarks, however, this might be the ticket. For information call (412) 255-2626 or visit www .city.pittsburgh.pa.us/parks.

The Waynesburg Hills

Venture into the extreme southwestern corner of Pennsylvania—dominated by Greene and Washington Counties and known officially as the Waynesburg Hills Section to geologists—and you are in a land of hills that roll one after another like waves on a green, grassy ocean.

This is sort of the anti–Allegheny Mountains. The weather is generally milder. Snowfalls are less common and less deep, and spring seems to come earlier, when ice still covers the lakes in some other parts of the state.

The result is that you see some species here that you might not elsewhere. Wildflowers like blue-eyed Mary and buckeye trees show up, as do sycamores, which flourish along some of the stream bottoms in this region.

Hikers walk their dog along the paved multiuse trail in Mingo Creek Park.

This is coal country—mining is a big part of the economy. But it's also pastoral. Getting to trailheads here takes you past fields of sheep, cattle, and horses.

You might see—or hear—some interesting wildlife as well. Coyotes populate every county in Pennsylvania now, but when their populations were first taking off, this is one of the places they first took hold. They don't pose a threat to humans, so you needn't fear them. You may never even see one; they're shy and elusive. But you can sometimes hear them howling if you hike early or late in the day. It's an eerie yet beautiful sound.

No matter what you see or hear, you can be sure that hiking in this part of the state means you may be climbing as often as not. There are no really high peaks in the region, though. The highest spot tops out at a modest 1,638 feet.

This is a country of narrow hilltops and steep-sloped, narrow valleys. In fact, it sometimes seems as if there is no flat country at all. Climb one hill and you'll find yourself descending a gully to climb another. And then another. And then another. It's no wonder that this area is more prone to landslides than any other part of the state.

But it has an appeal all its own. Spend time here—you'll be glad you did.

◀ *A view of the Monongahela River from the overlook at Friendship Hill National Historic Site.*

11 Mingo Creek Park

Start: Ebeneezer Bridge/Picnic Shelter No. 4
Distance: 3.1-mile loop
Approximate hiking time: 1.5–2 hours
Difficulty: Easy to moderate, with a few climbs
Trail surface: Dirt paths, gravel and paved roads, and a paved biking trail.
Seasons: Year-round
Other trail users: Horseback riders and mountain bikers
Canine compatibility: Dogs permitted, but they should be leashed.
Land status: County park
Fees and permits: No fees or permits required
Schedule: Open from dawn to dusk year-round

Maps: Trail map available by contacting Washington County Parks and Recreation; USGS Hackett
Trail contacts: Washington County Parks and Recreation, Courthouse Square, 100 West Beau Street, Suite 101, Washington 15301; (724) 228-6867; www.co.washington.pa.us/164/Parks-Recreation
Special considerations: Located in rural Washington County, Mingo Creek County Park sees a lot of horseback riders, and a portion of this hike shares a route open to them. It can be hiked at any time, but it's best in dry weather. When it's been wet and muddy, that horse traffic can create ruts.

Finding the trailhead: From Pittsburgh, take Interstate 79 south to exit 43 (Houston/Eighty Four). Turn right onto Route 519 south, then turn left onto Route 136 east. Go about 6 miles and turn left onto Sichi Hill Road. Turn right at the stop sign at the bottom of the hill, then take the next right into the park. *DeLorme: Pennsylvania Atlas and Gazetteer:* Page 71 C5. GPS coordinates N40 11.503 / W80 02.431

The Hike:

It wouldn't be fair, or even accurate, to say that no one knows about Mingo Creek Park. It attracts trout anglers each spring, hosts high school graduation parties each summer, and draws visitors to see its covered bridges each fall.

And no matter what time of year it is, there will be the occasional wedding party looking to get photographs.

But it's not known as a hiking mecca either. That's not to say no one hikes here. Locals do, for sure. But few people travel any great distance to explore Mingo Creek.

That's too bad. Tucked away in the rolling, pastoral hills of Washington County, Mingo Creek is a beautiful park, home to varied habitats and wildlife. White-tailed deer, squirrels, songbirds of all kinds, and even coyotes—rarely seen but sometimes heard at dusk and after—call this place home.

This hike allows you to experience all of that without having to tackle any especially rugged country.

To begin, park by Picnic Shelter No. 4 and the covered Ebeneezer Bridge. Hike up Pond Road. It's a gated maintenance road, closed to traffic, though there's the occasional park vehicle.

A waterfall located on an unnamed side trail in Mingo Creek Park.

In a little less than 0.1 mile there's an unmarked trail that goes off to the right. Follow this out a few hundred yards to see a really nice waterfall. It's especially pretty in spring, when there's more water flowing.

After checking out the waterfall, backtrack to the maintenance road and continue in the direction you were traveling. At 0.4 mile, look for the orange blazes marking Perimeter Trail.

Turn right and enter the woods on Perimeter Trail, which hikers share with bikers and horseback riders. It climbs steadily through young forest thick with grapevines until cresting a ridge at mile 0.6. As you start down the other side, notice an ancient beech tree and several mammoth oaks. They're magnificent in their antiquity, wise old kings whose reign dates to long-ago days when this woods was a pasture, as weathered fence posts here attest.

The trail next zigzags downhill until coming to a T at a trickle of a stream at mile 0.9. Turn left. Keep alert for white-tailed deer here.

Follow the orange blazes as the trail passes a gas line and crosses several gullies. The trail then loops around and, at mile 1.3, enters a stand of tall Austrian pines.

Meadows border the trail on the left starting at mile 1.7. This is another good spot to encounter deer, as well as turkeys.

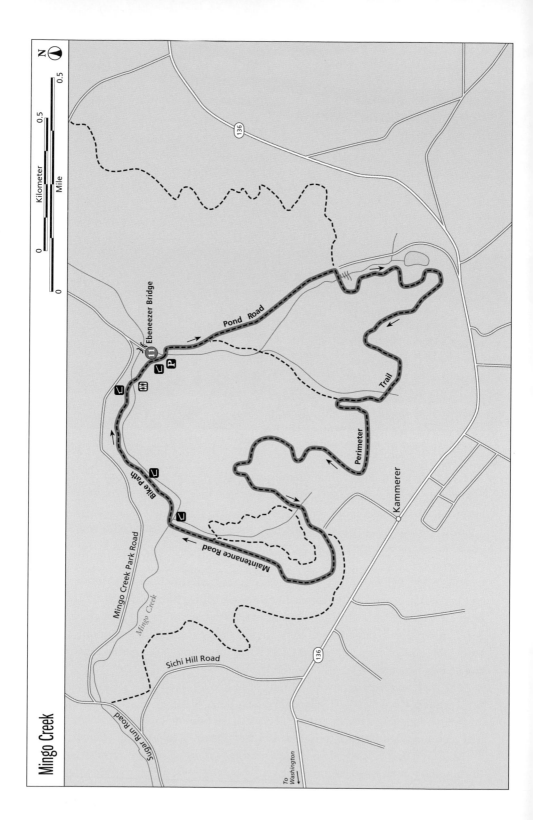

Mingo Creek

To Washington

Sugar Run Road

Sichi Hill Road

136

Mingo Creek

Mingo Creek Park Road

Mingo Creek

Bike Path

Maintenance Road

Kammerer

136

Perimeter Trail

Pond Road

Ebeneezer Bridge

N

Kilometer
0   0.5

Mile
0   0.5

When you reach mile 2.0, the trail meets a paved maintenance road. Turn right and follow the road downhill past a sign for Old Spring Trail, a parking lot, and a playground.

Just after crossing a bridge over Mingo Creek, at mile 2.6, turn right onto the paved walking/bike trail. It parallels Mingo Creek, buffered by tall sycamores in places. This is the busiest part of this hike as a general rule, with lots of dog walkers, joggers and, in season, anglers.

Follow the paved trail as it passes restrooms, picnic shelters, and benches, the latter of which make nice resting spots if you want to take in the scenery. Finally, recross Mingo Creek to wind up back at the start.

Mile and Directions

0.0 Start this hike by Picnic Shelter No. 4 and Ebeneezer Bridge, one of many covered bridges in Washington County. There are so many, in fact, that a festival to celebrate them is held each fall.

0.1 Come to a side trail on the left leading to a waterfall. Follow this, check out the falls, then return.

0.4 Turn right at the junction with Perimeter Trail, which is open to horseback riding and often marked by hoofprints.

0.6 Enter an old-growth forest, remarkable for some of the very large specimens to be found right at the trail's edge.

0.9 The trail Ts at a small stream, which can be dry in summer. Ignore the seemingly more obvious trail to the right and instead go left.

1.3 After climbing a hill, the trail enters a large stand of Austrian pines.

1.7 Look for a series of meadows on the left. These are good places to spot deer and turkeys. In April and May you might even be lucky enough to see a turkey gobbler strutting, tail fanned out wide, in an annual courtship display.

2.0 The trail meets with a paved maintenance road. Turn right and follow the road downhill.

2.6 Turn right onto the walking/biking trail just after crossing a bridge over Mingo Creek. The creek gets stocked with trout each year for the fishing season that begins in mid-April, so expect to see lots of anglers along the banks at that time of year.

3.1 Arrive back at the starting point, perhaps to wind up with a picnic lunch.

12 Buffalo Creek

Beginning at a neat little covered bridge, this is an easy hike along a gated road that follows Buffalo Creek on State Game Lands 232. Deer, waterfowl, squirrels, and other wildlife are common. A variety of songbirds can be found in the wetlands at the far end of the hike. The trail borders private property in some areas. That land is posted against trespassing, so be sure to stick to the road unless you're sure you are still on public ground.

Start: The Sawhill covered bridge on Route 221

Distance: 5.6 miles out and back

Approximate hiking time: 2–3 hours

Difficulty: Easy, with virtually no hills

Trail surface: Gated road

Seasons: Year-round

Other trail users: Hunters, bicyclists, and cross-country skiers

Canine compatibility: Dogs permitted; leashes not required

Land status: State game lands

Fees and permits: No fees or permits required

Schedule: Game lands open year-round, but this land was bought and is maintained using money from the sale of hunting licenses, so hunters have first use of the land. If you're planning to come here with an organized group, you need approval from the Pennsylvania Game Commission beforehand, particularly at certain times of year.

Maps: A map of State Game Lands 232, and a listing of game lands regulations, can be found at www.pgc.pa.gov/HuntTrap/StateGameLands/Pages/default.aspx. USGS West Middletown

Trail contacts: Pennsylvania Game Commission, Southwest Region Office, 4820 Route 711, Bolivar 15923; (724) 238-9523; www.pgc.state.pa.us

Special considerations: This area is very popular with hunters, primarily from October through late January and again from late April to late May. If you want to hike here at those times of year, it's best to do so on Sunday, when most hunting is prohibited.

Finding the trailhead: Exit Interstate 70 at Taylorstown onto Route 221 north. Go 6 miles to the Sawhill covered bridge on the left, and park there. *DeLorme: Pennsylvania Atlas & Gazetteer:* Page 70 C2. Trailhead GPS coordinates: N40 10.808 / W80 24.992

The Hike

Any number of wildlife species in Pennsylvania might qualify as cute when young or as majestic when they've reached adulthood. Black bears, white-tailed deer, bobcats, ospreys, red-winged blackbirds, red foxes—all would have their fans. Few people, if any, love the lowly opossum, though.

With their long, pointy snout, scaly tail that resembles a rat's, and coarse dirty-white fur, opossums won't win any beauty contests. Their habit of "playing possum" when attacked—which can involve falling over as if dead and excreting a musky odor—isn't overly endearing either.

A look at the countryside out the window of the covered bridge at the Buffalo Creek trailhead.

These are unique animals in their own right, however. Females give birth to tiny young—a litter of five to thirteen might fit in a tablespoon—that they carry around in a pouch, much like a kangaroo. At nine weeks the young emerge to ride around on their mother's back.

Most impressively, opossums are simply survivors. They will eat just about anything and can live in almost any habitat, so they're here to stay.

One place that you can surely find them is on State Game Lands 232 near Taylorstown. This is a mecca for people looking for more glamorous species, but if you walk the gated road that leads from the Sawhill covered bridge to a wetlands at another gate, you'll often spot opossum prints. They're especially distinctive when the toes of the front feet splay out in soft mud or snow to leave a star-shaped track.

The trail here leads up a small hill then drops down the opposite side. At 0.2 mile you'll come to a Y; turn right and cross the bridge. The trail then begins to parallel Buffalo Creek, where you can often spot ducks of various kinds.

A secondary road enters from the right at 0.6 mile. Continue past the road; 0.1 mile farther, at a bend in the road, look for an interesting rock face on the right.

One more road comes in, again from the right, at 0.8 mile. Bypass this road as well. You'll pass a number of sycamores where the creek runs close to the road and a broad floodplain where the stream is farther away.

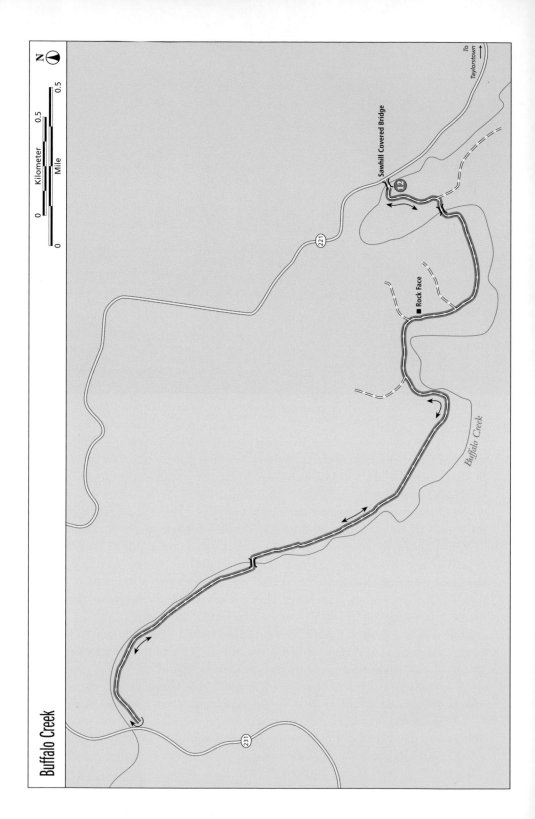

Buffalo Creek

N

Kilometer
0   0.5

Mile
0   0.5

221

Sawhill Covered Bridge

12

Rock Face

Buffalo Creek

231

To Taylorstown

The covered bridge at the trailhead for this Buffalo Creek hike on State Game Lands 232.

A third road comes in from the right at 1.4 miles. Skip this as you did the others and continue, looking in the dirt and mud of the road for animal tracks. Besides opossum tracks, you'll often see those left by raccoons, deer, foxes, and squirrels.

Mile 1.9 brings the only eyesore in this area. A concrete bridge that crosses over the creek sits covered in graffiti. Once you cross the bridge, the property on the left side of the road is posted against trespassing. On the right side, on the hillside that rises above the creek, you'll see some more interesting exposed rock.

You'll come to a Game Commission gate at 2.3 miles. Go around it and walk along the edge of a wetland area, where groups like Ducks Unlimited and the National Wild Turkey Federation have partnered to provide habitat for wildlife.

When you get to the road, turn and retrace your steps back to your vehicle.

Miles and Directions

0.0 Start by parking in the small lot near the Sawhill covered bridge.

0.2 The trail Ys. Go right and cross a bridge, but not before peeking into the creek below.

0.5 Bypass an impressive stand of evergreens on the right.

0.7 Also on the right, at a spot where the trail bends to the left, look for a rock formation.

1.4 Another gravel road comes in from the right. Ignore it and continue walking straight.

1.9 Cross a graffiti-covered bridge that will take you from the right bank of Buffalo Creek to the left.

2.3 Walk around a Game Commission gate that keeps motor vehicles off this road.

2.8 The trail ends when it meets a local road. Turn around here and retrace your steps.

5.6 Arrive back at the covered bridge.

13 Ryerson Station State Park

This is a pleasant hike through a park that never gets too crowded. It's tucked in the hills of Greene County in extreme southwestern Pennsylvania, near the West Virginia border. The park is definitely worth the trip, however. Sights you'll see include an old cemetery that, despite being hidden in the woods, is well maintained; some ancient trees; and lots of wildlife.

Start: The parking lot for Picnic Pavilion No. 2 in the Maple Grove day-use area.
Distance: 5.3-mile lollipop
Approximate hiking time: 2.5–3 hours.
Difficulty: Easy to moderate, with a few hills
Trail surface: Dirt paths with a short walk on one local roadway
Seasons: Year-round; best hiked April to October
Other trail users: Hunters and cross-country skiers

Canine compatibility: Leashed dogs permitted
Land status: State park
Fees and permits: No fees or permits required
Maps: Map available by contacting Ryerson Station State Park; USGS Wind Ridge
Trail contacts: Ryerson Station State Park, 361 Bristoria Road, Wind Ridge 15380-1258; (724) 428-4254; www.dcnr.state.pa.us/state parks/parks/ryersonstation.aspx
Special considerations: Portions of this hike run through areas open to hunting.

Finding the trailhead: Take Interstate 79 south to Route 21 and follow it west to the park entrance. *DeLorme: Pennsylvania Atlas & Gazetteer:* Page 84 A2. Trailhead GPS coordinates: N39 53.009 / W80 26.973

The Hike

Exactly what it was that took the life of little Susanna J. Grim has long been lost to the fog of history. Sickness? Primitive living conditions? An accident?

We do know that she died April 13, 1859, at the age of five years, two months, and ten days. We can imagine the pain felt by her parents, who nonetheless found solace in their faith.

"Our sweet little children have gone to mansions above yonder sky," reads Susanna's tombstone, "to gaze at the beautiful throne of Him who is seated on high."

Her final resting place—Chess Cemetery, where her marker is surrounded by others bearing names like Paron and Chess, some of them modern looking, others little more than weathered rectangles of stone—is one of the highlights of hiking Ryerson Station State Park.

This hike starts near Pavilion No. 2. Start up Fox Feather Trail and travel about 400 feet. There you'll turn right onto Lazear Trail.

At 0.2 mile you'll come to a white oak thought to be 300 years old. As the sign there explains, this "Wolf Tree" was likely the only tree to sprout in a field that existed at that time. It grew to shade out all competition, thereby ensuring its own survival.

A trail junction at Ryerson Station State Park. Crossing the bridge here leads to a short walk along the road.

Look around the woods here and you'll see several other trees that probably fall into this category.

Moving on, at 0.3 mile you'll see some signs warning of poison ivy, but the trail is very well maintained, so by keeping to the path you should be fine. Just ahead, Lazear Trail meets Orchard Trail on the left. Turn right to stay on Lazear.

At 0.6 mile you'll pass an overlook that gives you a nice view of the valley 424 feet below and some shagbark hickories, identifiable by the way their bark peels away from their trunks in vertical strips.

Mile 1.1 brings you to a junction with Tiffany Ridge Trail. Go right to stay on Lazear Trail, avoiding an unmarked trail that drops into a gully on your right 0.1 mile farther on.

Stay on Lazear, past where Tiffany Ridge Trail comes in again on the left at 1.4 miles, and where Fox Feather Trail comes in from the left at 1.5 miles. You'll stay on Lazear until you turn right onto Iron Bridge Trail.

Greene County has long been home to large numbers of deer, squirrels, turkeys, and coyotes, but for decades black bears were almost unheard of here. A few passed through occasionally, but they never took up residence. That's changed. A small population of bears now lives here year-round, so if you keep your eyes open, you just might get a glimpse of the county's newest wildlife resident.

A robin spotted along Lazear Trail.

The trail passes some cattails surrounding a swampy slough. Look for turkey vultures here, either soaring overhead, their wings forming a V, or in the trees looking for carrion.

At 1.9 miles you'll come to the Iron Bridge itself. Here the park map suggests that you can keep the bridge and the stream—the North Fork of Dunkard Fork of Wheeling Creek—on your left and proceed along the Pine Box Trail.

In reality, though, this portion of the Pine Box Trail no longer exists. Instead, turn left here, cross the Iron Bridge, and then turn right on Bristoria Road. Walk 0.6 mile—being careful, as there's not a lot of berm—and then enter the woods on the left where Pine Box Trail remains.

Start uphill on the moss-covered pathway—it feels as though you're walking on thick carpet—and at 3.4 miles you'll come to a Y. The Pine Box Trail goes left, and you'll want to take that way eventually. First, though, go straight to visit the Chess Cemetery.

Back on Pine Box, follow the hillside past a power line and around a couple of the deep gullies common here. When the trail brings you to the base of the power line, turn left and return to Bristoria Road. Cross the road, recross the Iron Bridge, and turn right onto the Iron Bridge Trail again.

This time, though, when you get back to the intersection of the Iron Bridge and Lazear Trails at 4.4 miles, turn right on Lazear. You'll find some hardwoods on your left and a view of what was Duke Lake on your right. At 4.8 miles you'll come to what is a confusing trail junction. Bearing right will take you around a field's edge, past a picnic area, and back to the parking lot where your hike began.

Ryerson Station State Park

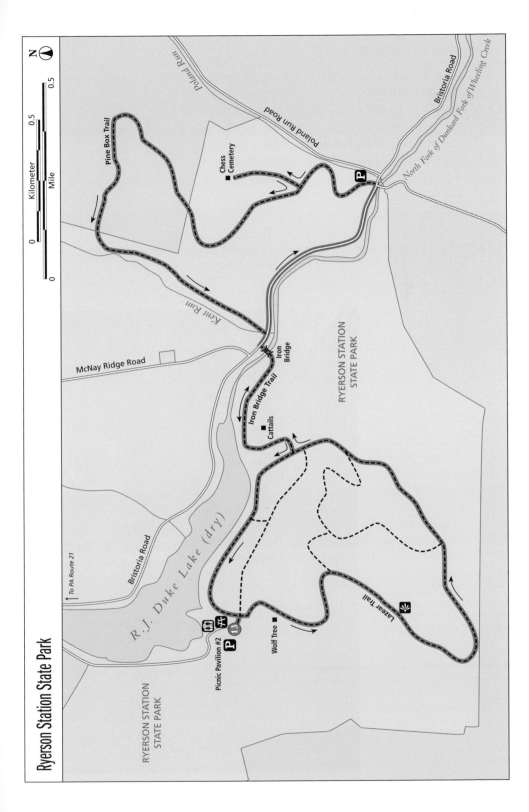

Miles and Directions

0.0 Start at the trailhead by Pavilion No. 2. A "you are here" type of sign at the edge of the lot marks the trailhead.

0.2 Look on the right for the park's "wolf tree," which is marked with a sign.

0.6 Come to what once was an overlook of Duke Lake. Now that the lake is drained, it provides a pastoral view of the valley instead.

1.1 Bypass the Tiffany Ridge Trail, which comes in on the left.

1.9 At the junction with the Iron Bridge Trail, turn right and follow the creek until you come to the Iron Bridge itself.

3.4 A small spur leads to the Chess Cemetery. This worthwhile side hike offers a glimpse into some local history.

4.4 After retracing your steps for a bit, you'll find yourself back at the junction of the Iron Bridge and Lazear Trails. Turn right and follow Lazear back to close the loop.

5.3 Arrive back at Picnic Pavilion No. 2.

A "wolf" tree in Ryerson Station State Park.

14 Friendship Hill National Historic Site

This is an easy to moderate hike, with a few short but steep hills. Wildlife—notably white-tailed deer, gray and fox squirrels, and songbirds—are abundant throughout the grounds, and you'll have the chance to get some nice views of the Monongahela River. What makes this hike unique, however, is the opportunity to visit the Gallatin House, where you can get a guided tour, watch a video presentation, and learn a lot about an important if little-known man from America's past.

Start: The parking lot near the Gallatin House Visitor Center
Distance: 4.0-mile loop
Approximate hiking time: 2 hours
Difficulty: Easy to moderate, with a few climbs and descents
Trail surface: A short section of paved sidewalk followed by a dirt path
Seasons: Year-round
Other trail users: Cross-country skiers in winter
Canine compatibility: Leashed dogs permitted
Land status: National Park Service historic site
Fees and permits: No fees or permits required
Schedule: The Albert Gallatin House is open 9:00 a.m. to 5:00 p.m. daily April through October; Saturday and Sunday only through winter.
Maps: A map of hiking trails on the grounds and a brochure describing Friendship Hill is available by contacting Friendship Hill National Historic Site. USGS Masontown
Trail contacts: Friendship Hill National Historic Site, 223 New Geneva Road, Point Marion 15474; visitor information: (724) 725-9190; park headquarters: (724) 329-5512; www.nps.gov/frhi
Special considerations: Hunting is not permitted on the site grounds, so this is a good place to hike on weekdays and on Saturdays in the fall.

Finding the trailhead: Take US Highway 119 south from Uniontown to Point Marion. Turn onto Route 166 north and go 3 miles to the park entrance. *DeLorme: Pennsylvania Atlas & Gazetteer:* Page 85 B6. Trailhead GPS coordinates: N39 46.645 / W79 55.862

The Hike

Tragedy made Albert Gallatin an American hero of sorts.

Born in Geneva, Switzerland, he traveled to America and then, with his new bride, to the edge of what was then the frontier in southwestern Pennsylvania. He settled on the banks of the Monongahela River—calling the area New Geneva—in 1789 and laid plans to manufacture firearms, glass, and other items for fellow settlers.

Not long after he arrived, though, his wife died—perhaps in childbirth, though no one knows for sure. Devastated, he began dabbling in politics. After a while, he remarried.

His second wife wanted no part of living full-time on the edge of civilization, however. As a result, Gallatin spent much of his remaining years away from New Geneva, living in the nation's capital.

A look at the grounds of Friendship Hill National Historic Site from the porch of the Gallatin mansion.

In the process, he became one of the most important men in America. Gallatin served thirteen years as secretary of the US Treasury under presidents Jefferson and Madison, funding the Louisiana Purchase and the Lewis and Clark expedition.

He always maintained his frontier home, though, and even added onto it more than once. Today that home is maintained by the National Park Service. You can stop by, learn a little history, then hike the attractive grounds.

This hike begins at the Gallatin House. Pass under the archway between the main house and a later addition. At 0.2 mile you'll come to a gazebo and overlook of the river, known locally as the Mon.

Follow the green-blazed Main Loop Trail to a meadow and at 0.25 mile turn right. You'll shortly reenter the woods and at 0.4 mile come to Sophia's Grave, where Gallatin's first wife was buried.

Pass a small pond often full of frogs, cross a bridge, and at 0.5 mile bypass the red-blazed Meadow Loop. You'll bypass the Meadow Loop again at 0.8 mile then descend steep, narrow steps, heading toward the Monongahela. This is where you'll find the one eyesore along this hike: piles of tires dumped in the woods just past the site boundary.

Turn right to put the tires at your back and follow the Main Loop Trail as it parallels the river, where you might spot a deer, an angler, or some of the very industry that Gallatin foresaw locating here centuries earlier. The trail is wide and flat in this section, offering easy walking.

The Gallatin mansion at Friendship Hill National Historic Site.

Mile Markers 1.9, 2.0, and 2.1 bring you to Ys in the trail; stay to the left, on the trails closer to the river, each time. At 2.6 miles you come to a junction with the New Geneva Spur Trail. Turn right, almost doubling back, to follow the green blazes of the Main Loop Trail.

At 2.8 miles you'll pass a small cemetery that's worth a peek. At 3.1 miles pass the School Spur, where the excited yells of children playing soccer and football will break the quiet.

At 3.3 miles you'll cross a bridge over Ice Pond Run. Turn right onto the green-blazed Ice Pond Run Loop and pass a marker explaining the impacts of acid mine drainage, visible as orange water here. Notice a field on your left. At 3.8 miles you'll

FESTIFALL

Each year on the last full weekend in September, Friendship Hill National Historic Site hosts a two-day "FestiFall." Visitors get to celebrate life as it was in Albert Gallatin's day by sampling foods like ham-and-bean soup, johnnycake, pulled-beef sandwiches, and popcorn popped over an open fire. The event always includes historical craft demonstrators, including quilters, coopers, pewter casters, soap makers, leatherworkers, seamstresses, furniture makers, and rug braiders. There's even period music and a military encampment. Best of all, admission is free and shuttle service is provided from the parking area.

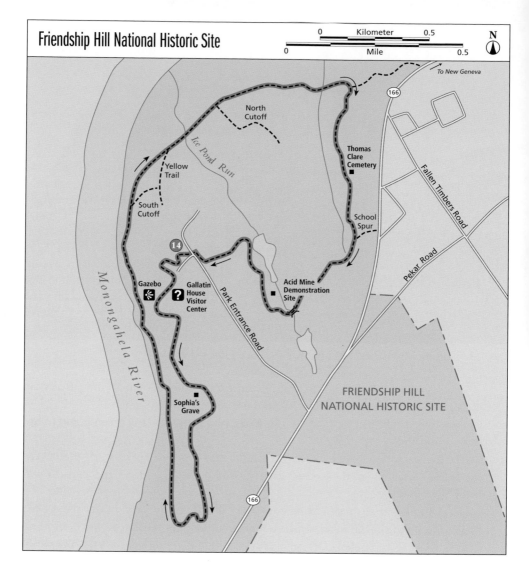

Friendship Hill National Historic Site

North Cutoff

Ice Pond Run

Yellow Trail

South Cutoff

Monongahela River

14

Gazebo

Gallatin House Visitor Center

Park Entrance Road

Sophia's Grave

166

Thomas Clare Cemetery

School Spur

Acid Mine Demonstration Site

To New Geneva

166

Fallen Timbers Road

Pekar Road

FRIENDSHIP HILL NATIONAL HISTORIC SITE

turn left into this field and walk its edge back to the park entrance road. Turn right and return to the parking lot. Watch for squirrels and deer along the way, especially early and late in the day.

Miles and Directions

0.0 Start at the trailhead, which means going from the main parking lot up the side sidewalk to the Gallatin House.

0.2 Shortly after walking beyond the Gallatin House, you'll come to a gazebo and an overlook offering a view of the Monongahela River.

0.4 It's not much to see, sort of a cut-stone foundation, but here is Sophia's Grave, final resting spot of Albert Gallatin's first wife.

2.0 At a cut in the hillside, cross Ice Pond Run, a tiny stream that goes almost dry in the hottest months.

2.8 Look on the left for Clare Cemetery, an overgrown but interesting highlight of the hike.

3.3 Recross Ice Pond Run at a spot where the impacts of acid mine drainage are documented.

3.8 Turn left at the junction with open meadow, being sure to watch for both deer and gray and fox squirrels here.

4.0 Arrive back at the parking area.

Honorable Mentions

N. Hillman State Park

Hillman is technically a state park, but it was leased to the Pennsylvania Game Commission some time ago for ninety-nine years. The commission is to manage the property as a game lands, meaning largely for hunters and wildlife. Local mountain bikers have established a number of trails on this Washington County tract, however, that when combined with some gated roads, offer good hiking. For information call (724) 899-2200 or visit www.dcnr.state.pa.us/stateparks/parks/hillman.aspx. You can find a map of the park and its trails at www.friendsofraccoon.com.

O. Ryerson Station State Park (Additional Trails)

There are a lot of possible loop hikes you can make in Ryerson Station State Park, one of which was described earlier in the book. There is a brand-new 1.2-mile trail there that you can try. Cross the Iron Bridge from Bristoria Road and turn left. The trail follows the path of what was the Pine Box Trail for a few hundred yards, then turns right into the woods and winds around before joining the Lazear Trail. For information call (724) 428-4254 or visit www.dcnr.state.pa.us/stateparks/parks/ryersonstation.aspx.

P. Warrior Trail

The Warrior Trail is a 70.0-mile footpath that stretches from Greene County in extreme southwestern Pennsylvania into West Virginia. It follows a trade route taken by Native Americans for as long as 5,000 years. The trail runs across private property for its entire length, but a guidebook available from the association that manages the trail tells you where you can find shelter, get water, and more. For information contact the Warrior Trail Association Inc., PO Box 103, Waynesburg 15370-0103.

The Allegheny Mountains

I f you want to experience mountain hiking in western Pennsylvania, you've got to head for the Alleghenies. Located east and south of Pittsburgh, they take in all of Somerset County and parts of Westmoreland, Fayette, Cambria, Indiana, Blair, and Bedford Counties.

The ridges—the Allegheny Mountain Section, to geologists—are often exposed hard rock, while the valleys are wide and undulating. The peaks are high, too. These mountains are among the highest in the state—indeed, the highest point in Pennsylvania, Mount Davis (elevation 3,213 feet), is located here. The going can be accordingly steep. The difference between the ridge crests and adjacent valley lowlands can be as much as 1,000 feet.

Late afternoon sun filters through the trees along Mill Run Trail in Quebec Run Wild Area.

The start of the Blair Brothers Railroad Grade, as seen through some of the mountain laurel that borders the trail.

That means that if you plan to hike here, expect some potentially challenging—read lung-busting—climbs. But they're not all that way. Whereas in eastern Pennsylvania the mountains are more on edge, one stacked after another, here the rocky ridges are often round and broad. If you get up high and stay there, the walking can be comparatively mild. The area around Mount Davis is a prime example of that.

You have to be prepared for differences in weather, though. Air temperatures are generally several degrees cooler in these mountains than in any of the surrounding country. Snowfalls can be significantly higher, too. A day of bare ground in Pittsburgh might mean 2 or 3 feet of snow on the Laurel and Chestnut Ridges.

Hardwood forests of oak and cherry predominate, with lots of hemlocks and mountain laurel thrown in. Wildlife species like black bears—they began their expansion into western Pennsylvania here nearly three decades ago—and timber rattlesnakes not as common elsewhere around Pittsburgh are abundant here.

There's some real room to roam here, too. Much of the public property found in this region of the state is in these mountains.

All in all, this is a fine place to get outside, especially if you want a little taste of wilderness close to home.

15 Laurel Hill State Park

This hike can be challenging if you do it end to end at one time. The Lake Trail portion, which clings to the steep hillside above Laurel Hill Lake, can be particularly tough, so you have to exercise some care there. Elsewhere the trail is relatively mild, with the sections leading to the dam on Jones Mill Run and the portion paralleling Laurel Hill Creek where it enters the lake well worth the effort.

Start: At the main parking lot near Picnic Area No. 3, opposite Group Camp 8

Distance: 7.1-mile loop

Approximate hiking time: 4 hours

Difficulty: Moderate to difficult, with the Lake Trail in particular very challenging

Trail surface: Dirt trail, with short pieces on unimproved roads

Seasons: Year-round; best hiked April to October

Other trail users: Cross-country skiers

Canine compatibility: Leashed dogs permitted

Land status: State park

Fees and permits: No fees or permits required

Maps: Map available by contacting Laurel Hill State Park; USGS Bakersville, Seven Springs, and Rockwood

Trail contacts: Laurel Hill State Park, 1454 Laurel Hill Park Road, Somerset 15501-5629; (814) 445-7725; www.dcnr.state.pa.us/state parks/parks/laurelhill.aspx

Special considerations: Portions of Laurel Hill State Park are open to hunting, so wear orange during those seasons.

Finding the trailhead: Laurel Hill State Park is located just off Route 31 near Bakersville. Take Route 3037 from Route 31 to the park road. *DeLorme: Pennsylvania Atlas & Gazetteer:* Page 73 D5. Trailhead GPS coordinates: N39 59.882 / W79 14.403

The Hike

Between 1933 and 1945, the young men of the Civilian Conservation Corps (CCC)—the out-of-work but ablebodied backbone of the nation—built roads, bridges, and buildings in state parks all across Pennsylvania.

Nowhere is that work more evident than at Laurel Hill State Park in the Laurel Highlands of Somerset County. The park was one of five in the state designated as a recreational demonstration area by the National Park Service. As such, it was given extra attention in terms of reforestation and the development of camping and picnicking areas.

Today much of that work is still evident, with one of the most beautiful examples being the stone dam on Jones Mill Run, which you see on this hike.

To begin, park in the large parking area near Picnic Area No. 3, near the swimming beach. Walk back to the main park road and turn right (north) and follow it for 0.3 mile. Turn left onto the gated road leading to Group Camp 8, another remnant of the CCC era.

A grave marker in Jones Scott Singo Cemetery.

Right away you'll pass the Jones Scott Singo Cemetery, which has graves dating to 1813. Recently restored by the Friends of Laurel Hill, and with a history of the plot posted nearby, it's worth a few minutes before you move on.

When you're ready, follow the road into the camp until you reach a Y. Turn right on the orange-blazed snowmobile trail. Just past a water tower on your left, follow the sign for Ridge Trail.

At 0.8 mile turn right to follow the Pumphouse Trail. This will take you through a forest of beech, oak, and cherry along Jones Mill Run.

Mile 1.1 brings a bridge and a left turn onto Tram Road Trail. You'll soon cross Jones Mill Run three more times—without the benefit of bridges—the last coming at the foot of the dam on Jones Mill Run. The rough-cut rectangular stones that form this structure look like blocks of dark chocolate fudge stacked tightly together, with the water of Jones Mill Run pouring over them. It's stunning, really, and a perfect place to stop, snap a photo, and enjoy the solitude. If poems aren't composed here, they should be.

When you're ready to move on, put the dam at your back and follow Tram Road Trail until it reaches a T at 1.5 miles. There turn left where the Pumphouse, Martz, and Tram Road Trails all run together for a while. Follow that wide, relatively flat trail until Tram Road Trail splits off to the left; continue right on Pumphouse Trail, going uphill.

At 2.3 miles you'll come to another T; go left onto Martz Trail and follow it for 0.3 mile until you come to the dirt Beltz Road. Turn right and go 0.3 mile, then turn right onto Bobcat Trail. This trail is generally easy to follow, ultimately leading through some thick mountain laurel.

Bobcat runs into Buck Run Road at Camp Conestoga, a Cub Scout camp, at 3.9 miles. Turn left onto the road, walk past the dining hall, and at 4.0 miles turn right onto Hemlock Trail. When this trail Ys a short time later, go left, downhill toward the creek. You'll walk through a stand of virgin hemlocks and see some excellent views of Laurel Hill Creek, which offers tremendous fishing if you're interested in packing a rod and willing to use artificial lures.

At 4.6 miles Hemlock Trail meets the main park road. Turn left, cross the bridge, and walk down the stairs leading to Lake Trail.

This is where the hiking becomes more difficult. Lake Trail follows the east side of Laurel Hill Lake and is very narrow and steep over the course of the next mile, with some severe drop-offs to the water below. A walking stick is a good idea.

By the time the trail gets to the spillway at 5.8 miles, it levels out. Continue along the trail, near the border with private property on your right, until you hit the paved road (Route 3029) at 6.0 miles.

Turn right onto this road, cross the bridge over Laurel Hill Creek, then climb over the guardrail to follow the creek up the other side along an unnamed angler's path. When you reach the spillway at 6.7 miles, turn left up the paved access road and then right to follow the walkway past the swimming beach.

You'll come to the park's concession stand. Treat yourself to an ice-cream cone or a cool drink, then turn left and climb through the parking lot back to your car.

Markers pay tribute to the military service of those buried in Jones Scott Singo Cemetery.

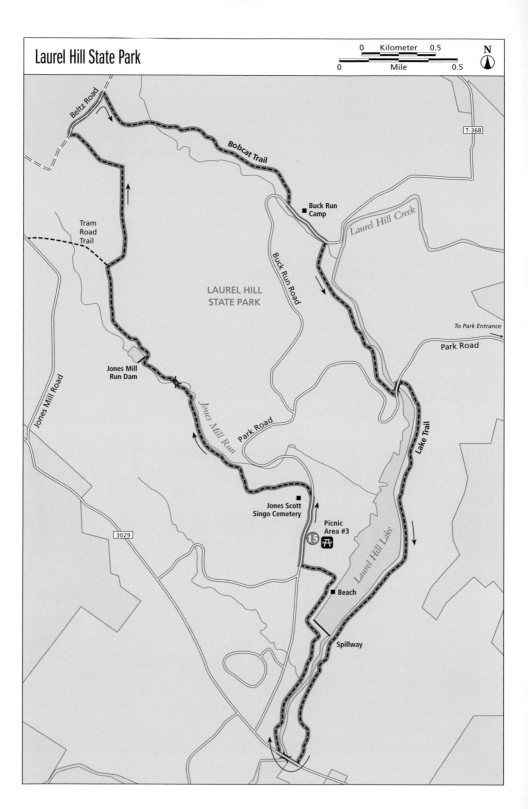

Laurel Hill State Park

Beltz Road

Bobcat Trail

Buck Run Camp

Laurel Hill Creek

T-368

Tram Road Trail

LAUREL HILL STATE PARK

Buck Run Road

To Park Entrance

Park Road

Jones Mill Road

Jones Mill Run Dam

Jones Mill Run

Park Road

Lake Trail

Jones Scott Singo Cemetery

3029

Picnic Area #3

15

Laurel Hill Lake

Beach

Spillway

Kilometer
Mile

N

Miles and Directions

0.0 Start at the parking lot, a tiered affair, near Picnic Area No. 3.

0.3 Pass Jones Scott Singo Cemetery, which will be on your left, inside a small fence and gate. Some printed material here tells the tale of the site.

1.1 Cross a small footbridge over Jones Mill Run at the Tram Road Trail junction.

1.5 Come to the beautiful CCC dam on Jones Mill Run. A bench and some large stones make great seats if you want to stop and have lunch, read a book, or just relax.

2.6 At the Beltz Road junction, turn right onto the road.

3.9 Pass Camp Conestoga's Cub Scout dining hall on the left. Expect to see Scouts here in June and July.

5.1 Look on your right for what remains of a crumbling lean-to shelter on Lake Trail.

5.8 The Laurel Hill Lake spillway will be on your right. It's a great spot to see herons if there aren't any anglers around.

6.7 You're on the opposite side of the spillway, just a stone's throw from where you were before. Get here by following an unmarked angler's path.

7.1 Pass the park beach and swimming area on your right and climb a short ways back to the parking area.

GREEN TIP
Recycle your old gear by giving it to someone or an organization that will reuse it.

16 Wolf Rocks Trail

A lot of hikes promise to lead to scenic overlooks. Often, though, the views are somewhat obstructed by trees. That's not the case with Wolf Rocks Trail, which leads to a rocky outcrop nearly 100 feet wide that showcases a magnificent expanse of the Linn Run Valley. The view is particularly stunning in summer and fall, but even in winter, when the mountains are blanketed in snow, this is an amazing site.

Start: Laurel Summit Picnic Area
Distance: 4.5-mile lollipop
Approximate hiking time: 2–2.5 hours
Difficulty: Easy to moderate, with flat terrain but occasionally wet conditions and rocky trail surface
Trail surface: Dirt paths
Seasons: Year-round
Other trail users: Cross-country skiers and mountain bikers
Canine compatibility: Leashed dogs permitted
Land status: State forest
Fees and permits: No fees or permits required
Maps: Forest map available by contacting Forbes State Forest; park map available by

contacting Laurel Summit State Park; USGS Ligonier
Trail contacts: Laurel Summit State Park, c/o Linn Run, Rector 15677-0050; (724) 238-6623; www.dcnr.state.pa.us/stateparks/parks/laurelsummit.aspx. Forbes State Forest, Bureau of Forestry, Forestry District #4, PO Box 519, Laughlintown 15655; (724) 238-1200; www.dcnr.state.pa.us/forestry/stateforests/forbes.aspx
Special considerations: The trailhead can be difficult to reach in winter. Linn Run Road does not get plowed (for the sake of snowmobilers), and while Laurel Summit Road does get plowed, this area can get a lot of snow.

Finding the trailhead: Follow US Highway 30 east past Ligonier to the top of Laurel Summit. Turn right onto Laurel Summit Road and follow it about 5 miles to a T. Turn right and pull into the Laurel Summit State Park. *DeLorme: Pennsylvania Atlas & Gazetteer:* Page 73 C5. Trailhead GPS coordinates: N40 07.105 / W79 10.595

The Hike

The launch point for Wolf Rocks Trail is sort of deceiving. Situated in Laurel Summit State Park—which takes in all of 6 acres and consists of one pavilion, a restroom, and a gravel parking lot—it seems nondescript, to say the least.

The view at the end of this hike is nothing short of spectacular, however.

To begin, look for the sign for Wolf Rocks Trail at the edge of the parking lot. Right away you'll notice some sassafras growing here. There's also plenty of mountain laurel. The trail is flat but rocky, with roots stretching across it like hardened veins, so be careful not to stumble. In time you'll also encounter a lot of ferns, some of them growing waist high, giving sections of this hike an almost prehistoric feel.

Mountain laurel and rhododendron flourish along Wolf Rocks Trail,
with the peak of the bloom in early June.

A hiker smiles from behind some of the plentiful mountain laurel along Wolf Rocks Trail.

At 0.5 mile you'll come to an intersection with Wolf Rocks Loop Trail and Spruce Flats Trail. You'll return via Wolf Rocks Loop later, so ignore both of these turns for now and continue straight on Wolf Rocks Trail.

Mile 0.7 brings you to the first of several "bridges"—really elevated planks—built over wet spots in the trail. These welcome additions do wonders for keeping your feet dry and for preventing mountain bikers from creating ruts.

Pass a plot of ferns in a sun-drenched opening in the woods at 0.8 mile. At 1.2 miles the trail splits. Turn left at a red marker to stay on Wolf Rocks Trail. You should be able to seen a woven-wire fence, meant to keep deer out of an area foresters want to regenerate, on your right. If instead you find yourself on a logging road, you've missed the turn.

Look for an interesting rock formation on your left at 1.4 miles. Notice how greenbrier is trying to overtake the forest in this area.

The Wolf Rocks Loop Trail comes in on the left again at 1.9 miles. Bypass it for now. Also continue straight on Wolf Rocks Trail a few hundred yards farther on, when Bobcat Trail comes in from the right.

At 2.2 miles you'll come to Wolf Rocks, an outcropping of Pottsville sandstone roughly 2,600 feet above sea level. At that elevation, it's no surprise that there is evidence of frost cracks in the stone. There are signs of hikers having built a few fires here, too, but the area is remarkably free of litter and graffiti, so please keep it that way. Pack your trash out.

Wolf Rocks Trail

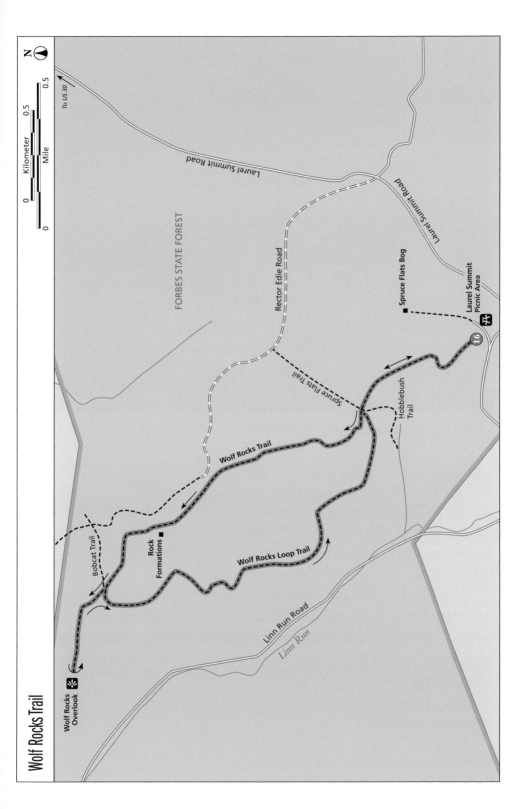

FORBES STATE FOREST

Laurel Summit Road

Laurel Summit Road

To US 30

Rector Edie Road

Spruce Flats Bog

Laurel Summit
Picnic Area

Spruce Flats Trail

Wolf Rocks Trail

Hobblebush
Trail

Bobcat Trail

Rock
Formations

Wolf Rocks Loop Trail

Linn Run Road

Linn Run

Wolf Rocks
Overlook

N

Kilometer
0   0.5

Mile
0   0.5

A view of the mountains of the Laurel Highlands from the Wolf Rocks overlook.

BIG BOG

If you're going to do this hike, also take the time to check out the Spruce Flats Wildlife Management Area, which takes in 305 acres by the picnic area. Its dominant feature—and the one everyone knows it for—is a 28-acre bog containing a variety of plants typically found much farther to the north, including the carnivorous pitcher plant.

No one knows for sure what created the bog. Perhaps glaciers had something to do with it. What is known is that lumbermen perpetuated its survival. Their cutting of the area's hemlocks—which they mistakenly called spruce—opened the door for subsequent fires that burnt away the debris on the forest floor, allowing the water table to reach the surface and creating the bog.

Time will eventually reclaim the forest, and the bog will disappear. For now, though, it's a sight worth seeing.

When you turn to go, backtrack to mile 2.5 until you can turn right onto Wolf Rocks Loop Trail. Greenbrier is superabundant along this trail, so there aren't many opportunities to wander off and explore without doing some serious bushwhacking.

You'll cross two small seeps at 2.7 miles. Continue until Wolf Rocks Loop meets again with Wolf Rocks at 4.0 miles. (Hobblebush Trail, an expert mountain biking trail, is also here.) Turn right onto Wolf Rocks Trail and walk it back to the starting point.

Miles and Directions

0.0   Start at the Laurel Summit Picnic Area, which has a pavilion in case you want to picnic before going home.

0.5   Come to a junction with Wolf Rocks Loop Trail on the left and Spruce Flats Trail on the right. Ignore both and continue straight.

0.7   Cross a small bridge that stands just inches off the ground yet will do a lot to keep your feet dry.

1.2   The trail turns left, away from a logging road. If you find yourself on a sunlit, grassy road, you've gone too far.

1.4   Look for rock formations on both sides of the trail.

1.9   Look on the left for the junction with Wolf Rocks Loop. Avoid it for now and stay straight.

1.92 To the right you'll see the junction with Bobcat Trail. Ignore it and stay straight.

2.2   Come to the highlight of the trail, the Wolf Rocks overlook, which offers a stunning view of the Laurel Mountains.

2.5   On your way back, turn right at the junction with Wolf Rocks Loop Trail.

4.0   At the junction with Wolf Rocks Trail, turn right and retrace your steps to close the loop.

4.5   Arrive back at the parking area and your vehicle.

17 Grove Run Trail

Despite being relatively short, this hike has enough climbs to get your attention. Add in a few waterfalls, a trail register that sometimes reads as funny as the script to a TV sitcom, and a section where the trail clings narrowly to a steep hill, and this is a fun walk. Because it starts and ends at a picnic area with water, restrooms, grills, and tables, it's a great hike to combine with a picnic.

Start: The Grove Run Picnic Area in Linn Run State Park
Distance: 3.8-mile loop
Approximate hiking time: 1.5–2 hours.
Difficulty: Moderate to difficult, with some challenging climbs
Trail surface: Dirt paths
Seasons: Year-round
Other trail users: Cross-country skiers and bicyclists in some places
Canine compatibility: Leashed dogs permitted
Land status: State park and state forest
Fees and permits: No fees or permits required
Schedule: Although the park is open year-round, the gate to the main parking area is

sometimes closed. In that case, there is a smaller spot for cars along Linn Run Road.
Maps: Maps available by contacting Linn Run State Park or Forbes State Forest; USGS Ligonier
Trail contacts: Linn Run State Park, PO Box 50, Rector 15677-0050; (724) 238-6623; www. dcnr.state.pa.us/stateparks/parks/linnrun. aspx. Forbes State Forest, Bureau of Forestry, Forestry District #4, PO Box 519, Laughlintown 15655; (724) 238-1200; www.dcnr.state. pa.us/forestry/stateforests/forbes.aspx.
Special considerations: This area is open to hunting and is very popular, especially in bear and deer seasons—late November and early December.

Finding the trailhead: Take US Highway 30 east past Ligonier. Turn south onto Route 381 to Rector, then left onto Linn Run Road. *DeLorme: Pennsylvania Atlas & Gazetteer:* Page 73 C5. Trailhead GPS coordinates: N40 09.064 / W79.13.613

The Hike

Linn Run State Park is a mountain playground, and has been for decades. The people who come here to picnic, hike, fish, hunt, or rent a cabin and vacation in the forest hail from all across western Pennsylvania and beyond.

Things weren't always that way, however. When the state purchased this land in the early part of the twentieth century—after it had been clear-cut and the regenerating forest burnt multiple times in fires sparked by embers from train engines—many thought it was little more than a wasteland.

Grove Run Trail near the Grove Run Picnic Area. ▶

A female downy woodpecker on a tree along Grove Run Trail.

No one thinks that anymore. To hike Grove Run Trail now is to walk under a canopy of oak and cherry; past waterfalls; and among deer, bears, foxes, and bobcats.

To start, pick up Grove Run at the far end of the picnic area of the same name. The trail starts out flat, following Grove Run upstream. It climbs a short hill at 0.3 mile and then largely levels out again to parallel the stream.

Mile 0.9 brings you to a bridge and Grove Run waterfall. Pretty even in dry years and the heat of summer, it's most impressive in spring, when snowmelt adds to the water flow. For about the next 0.25 mile, the trail is usually wet, too, as the runoff follows the trail as well as any hiker does. More worrisome, if you're not careful, is the stinging nettles that grow in this area. Their fine barbs are as irritating as their name would suggest. Stick to the trail to avoid them.

Look for a small waterfall on your left at 1.0 mile and another, trickling over a rock face, on the right at 1.1 miles. The trail then switches back on itself to climb. Notice all the greenbrier here, which is aggressively taking over the woods—climbing trees, covering the forest floor, and edging its way toward the trail.

Climb a little farther and at 1.4 miles come to a trail sign-in box. This is always worth a read. Mark and Anastasia announced their engagement here. A fifty-year-old

The black cherry trees that grow along Grove Run Trail and elsewhere in western Pennsylvania are an important source of food for wildlife. Seventy species of birds, black bears, raccoons, foxes, chipmunks, coyotes, squirrels, and other species all feast on their fruit.

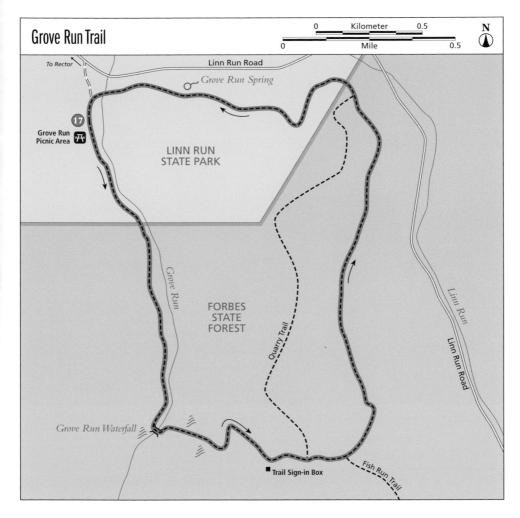

Grove Run Trail

0 Kilometer 0.5

0 Mile 0.5

N

To Rector

Linn Run Road

Grove Run Spring

Grove Run
Picnic Area

17

LINN RUN
STATE PARK

Grove Run

FORBES
STATE
FOREST

Quarry Trail

Linn Run

Linn Run Road

Grove Run Waterfall

Trail Sign-in Box

Fish Run Trail

novice hiker from Ohio noted that this was her first hike with her husband. Five "hermits" who claimed to have been wandering the forest for two years—Secret Squirrel, Muddobber, Lizard, Pirate, and Mongo—signed in. And at least one member of the "Beer Nutz" issued a warning: "Supplies low. Morale lower. Mutiny level high."

Leaving here, climb a little higher and you come to an intersection with Quarry Trail at 1.6 miles. Cross this road—popular with bicyclists and snowmobilers—to stay on Grove Run Trail.

Fish Run Trail breaks off to the right 0.3 mile farther. Stay left on Grove Run. The trail gets very rocky, with lots of ferns in evidence. It also gets narrow as it clings to the side of the mountain.

At 2.7 miles Linn Run Road becomes visible down the hill to the right. Stay on the trail, paralleling the road, until you cross Quarry Trail again at 2.9 miles. The trail bends to the left here, ultimately crossing over Grove Run itself on its way back to the picnic area and the starting point.

Fallen leaves make a colorful pallet in the shallow waters of Grove Run.

Miles and Directions

0.0 Park at the Grove Run Picnic Area and pick up the trail at the far end of the lot, behind a gate surrounded by a few boulders.

0.9 Bear left and cross a bridge over Grove Run, just below the stream's main waterfall.

1.1 Look on your right for a small, unnamed waterfall partially hidden by vegetation.

1.4 Come to a trail sign-in box where you can read about hikers who have come this way before, and leave your own message.

1.6 This point brings you to a junction with Quarry Trail—a wide, grassy pathway frequently used by bikers in summer and snowmobilers in winter. Cross straight over.

2.9 Cross Quarry Trail a second time, although here it's under the trees.

3.8 Finish back at Grove Run Picnic Area. The trail brings you to a fountain where you can get one last cool drink.

18 Conemaugh Gap

The second-most challenging portion of the Laurel Highlands Hiking Trail—a 70.0-mile backpacking trail—this hike includes a couple of serious climbs. The payoff comes in the form of multiple overlooks of the Conemaugh River. It's neat to see birds flying high above cars—and to be high enough to look down on all of them.

Start: The northern Laurel Highlands Hiking Trail trailhead in Seward
Distance: 7.2 miles out and back
Approximate hiking time: 3.5–4.5 hours
Difficulty: Moderate to difficult, with some long climbs on a trail that often hugs the edge of a bluff
Trail surface: Dirt path
Seasons: Year-round
Other trail users: Hunters
Canine compatibility: Dogs permitted; leashes not required
Land status: State park

Fees and permits: No fees or permits required
Maps: Park map available by contacting Laurel Hill State Park; USGS New Florence and Vintondale
Trail contacts: Laurel Hill State Park, 1454 Laurel Hill Park Road, Somerset 15501-5629; (814) 455-7725; www.dcnr.state.pa.us/state parks/parks/laurelhill.aspx
Special considerations: This section of the Laurel Highlands typically gets more snow than surrounding lowlands, so hiking the trail in winter can be especially challenging.

Finding the trailhead: Take US Highway 22 east from Pittsburgh. Exit onto Route 56 south at Armagh and go 3.9 miles to the parking area. *DeLorme: Pennsylvania Atlas & Gazetteer:* Page 73 A6. Trailhead GPS coordinates: N40 24.503 / W79 00.328

The Hike

You can't hike anywhere near the Conemaugh River without thinking of the great Johnstown Flood.

On May 31, 1899, the industrial town in western Cambria County was already full of water. The Conemaugh, as it was wont to do at least once every year, was overflowing its banks, forcing people to move their valuables into the upper reaches of their homes.

On this day, though, the unthinkable happened. The dam on Lake Conemaugh—a private, 2-mile-long, mile-wide lake for a prestigious club that included some of the region's and country's biggest names, like Andrew Carnegie of US Steel fame—burst. A wall of water and debris described by survivors as being 40 feet tall and half a mile wide roared into town.

The consequences were horrific. A total of 2,209 people lost their life. Some survivors were washed far downriver past Seward, where this hike begins.

The trail starts out relatively flat and is very well marked with yellow blazes. One hundred yards in, you'll come to an informational sign explaining a little bit about

Hikers heading into the Conemaugh Gap are asked to register upon embarking.

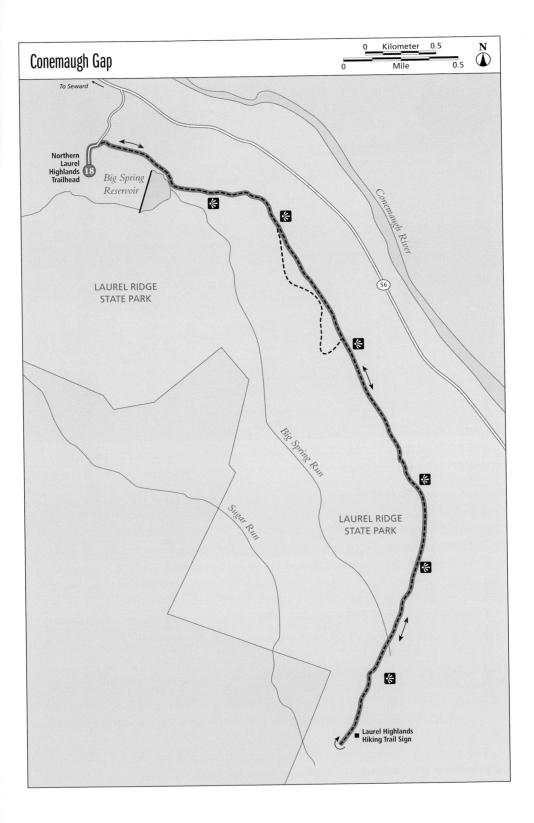

Conemaugh Gap

To Seward

Northern
Laurel
Highlands
Trailhead

18

Big Spring Reservoir

LAUREL RIDGE STATE PARK

Conemaugh River

56

Big Spring Run

Sugar Run

LAUREL RIDGE STATE PARK

Laurel Highlands
Hiking Trail Sign

0   Kilometer   0.5

0   Mile   0.5

N

Looking through greenbrier to take in view from a power line along the Laurel Highlands Hiking Trail at the Conemaugh Gap.

this end of the Laurel Highlands Hiking Trail. There's also a trail register here, with cards to be filled out. If you have a pen or pencil, fill out a card, even if you plan to be gone just a few hours.

At 0.2 mile you'll cross a forest road leading to Big Spring Reservoir, a local water supply. Continue following the yellow blazes and cross a power line at 0.7 mile. This offers some nice views, but nothing like what is yet to come. There's a good bit of greenbrier here, too, so be careful if you venture off the trail.

Descend into a valley with lots of oak trees and some interesting rock formations. At 1.1 miles you'll cross another forest road and follow the trail as it winds through some rhododendron so thick it almost forms a tunnel.

The trail brushes up against the forest road one more time at 1.5 miles. Follow the yellow blazes and you'll come to another power line at 1.6 miles. This one offers a view of a power plant to the right but a fantastic look at the Conemaugh Gorge on the left, where the vehicles in the valley look like Matchbox cars. Some large rocks piled up here add to the view.

The trail next follows the rim of the gorge, with more overlooks at 2.3 and 2.8 miles. You'll pass by the trail's Mile Marker 67 at 2.9 miles.

Shortly after climbing uphill, at 3.3 miles you get a nice view of the river. It's not as clear as the one on the power line, especially if the leaves are on the trees, but the river is as close here as anywhere.

The trail then winds farther into the woods, away from the river. At 3.6 miles you'll come to a sign explaining the rules of the Laurel Highlands Hiking Trail.

Stop here, turn, and retrace your steps to the car, being sure to examine the rock formations on the rim of the gorge, which are easier to appreciate from this direction.

Miles and Directions

0.0 Find the trailhead in Seward near the end of a cul-de-sac. A sign marks the trail here.

0.2 Look on the right for a glimpse of Big Spring Reservoir.

0.7 Cross under a power line that offers views of vehicles far below.

1.5 Skirt a forest road, which will be on your right. The trail nears it here but never actually crosses it.

1.6 Cross under another power line, this one marked by some giant boulders. The view in each direction is pretty special.

2.3 This point offers an overlook, but be careful of the steep hillside that falls away to the left.

2.8 Yet another view. Again, be careful of the hill. Falling here would mean sliding a long way in a hurry.

3.3 It's not an unobstructed view by any means, but this spot does give you a view of the Conemaugh River below.

3.6 The trail continues here, but when you come to a sign for the Laurel Highlands Hiking Trail, turn around and retrace your steps.

7.2 Arrive back at the parking lot and your car.

It's not uncommon to see turkey vultures—one of two species of vulture that inhabit Pennsylvania—soaring on the air currents above the gorge. You'll know one if you see it. In flight, when riding the currents, their wings form a deep V. Up close, they have no feathers on their heads or necks—the better to feast on carrion without getting too messy.

19 Mount Davis

Mount Davis is the highest point in Pennsylvania, with an elevation of 3,213 feet above sea level. Don't come here expecting to see a singular majestic peak, however. The area around Mount Davis is one big plateau, so while you can get a very nice view from an observation tower, this area is surprisingly flat. You also will see several streams and a unique spring and learn a little history of the area.

Start: The Mount Davis Picnic Area
Distance: 7.8-mile loop
Approximate hiking time: 3.5–4.5 hours
Difficulty: Moderate, with surprisingly few climbs but some areas of brushy trail
Trail surface: Dirt paths
Seasons: Year-round; best between April and October
Other trail users: Cross-country skiers, hunters, snowmobilers, and, increasingly, mountain bikers
Canine compatibility: Dogs permitted; leashes not required
Land status: State forest
Fees and permits: No fees or permits required

Maps: Trail map available by contacting Forbes State Forest; USGS Markleton
Trail contacts: Forbes State Forest, Bureau of Forestry, Forestry District #4, PO Box 519, Laughlintown 15655; (724) 238-1200; www.dcnr.state.pa.us/forestry/stateforests/forbes.aspx
Special considerations: This is the state's highest point and is, appropriately enough, a place of extremes. Annual temperatures range from minus 30 to 95 degrees Fahrenheit. It is not uncommon for winter snow depths to reach 3 to 4 feet—perhaps three times as deep as what you'll find at lower elevations. Frost has been observed at some point during every month of the year, too.

Finding the trailhead: Take the Pennsylvania Turnpike to the Somerset exit. Get on US Highway 219 south and follow it to Meyersdale. From Meyersdale take Route 2004 to the picnic area. *DeLorme: Pennsylvania Atlas & Gazetteer:* Page 87 B5. Trailhead GPS coordinates: N39 47.612 / W79 10.093

The Hike

Take one average-size NBA basketball player and put him in a room full of nonathletes, and he will seem tall. Put him in a room full of his counterparts from the court, and he'll seem, well, not such a giant after all.

That's the dilemma facing Mount Davis.

At 3,213 feet the highest point in the state, Mount Davis would tower over the Ohio River Valley to the west or the rich farm country of Lancaster County to the east. Located in central Somerset County as it is, though, it's just inches taller than some of the surrounding peaks.

The sign at Mount Davis Picnic Area in winter. There is often deep snow here, as this is the highest point in Pennsylvania. ▶

WELCOME TO
MT. DAVIS
PICNIC AREA
FORBES STATE FOREST
BUREAU OF FORESTRY

D.C.N.R.

Large stands of ferns carpet the forest floor, almost obscuring the trail around Mount Davis in spots.

Still, the greater Mount Davis Natural Area and Forbes State Forest offer wonderful opportunities to enjoy the kind of nature common to southwestern Pennsylvania's mountains.

To begin this hike, pick up High Point Trail near the western edge of the picnic area. At a little past the 0.1-mile mark, turn left onto Tub Mill Trail, which winds through an area dominated by boulders and ferns.

At 0.5 mile cross Shelter Rock Road to stay on Tub Mill Trail. Keep your eyes open for blazes here—the trail is very narrow and can be hard to pick up among the rocks and mountain laurel.

The trail begins to climb uphill at 1.7 miles. Watch for ruffed grouse; it's not uncommon to flush one or more of the birds in this area.

You'll pass some interesting rock formations at 2.1 miles. At 2.3 miles you'll come to some large hemlocks and a small stream, hidden by brush so that you hear it before you see it. Tub Mill Trail stays near the stream here, providing for a cool, shaded walk.

Mile 2.5 brings you to a spot where the trail runs up against the state forest boundary. Turn right and cross a small stream to stay on the trail. The junction with Timberslide Trail is just a couple hundred yards farther ahead. Turn left to stay on Tub Mill.

At 2.9 miles Tub Mill Trail ends at South Wolf Rock Road. Turn right and walk along the road up a slight grade. At 3.4 miles turn left and reenter the woods onto Laurel Run Trail. Follow Laurel Run for 1.0 mile, then turn right onto Wolf Rock Trail, which makes its way through some laurel.

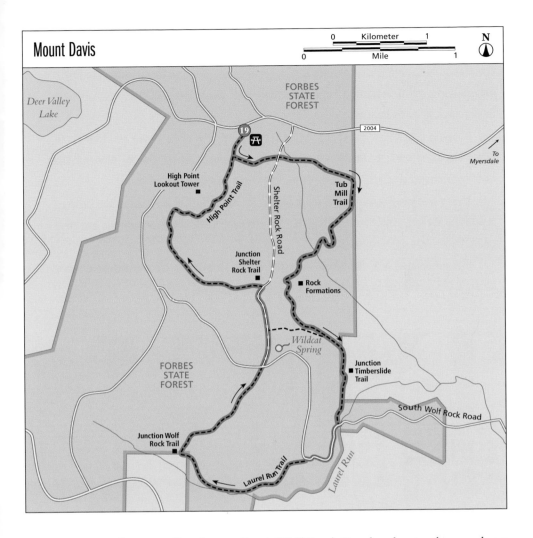

At 5.2 miles cross directly over South Wolf Rock Road and enter the woods on Shelter Rock Road, a gated, grassy Forest Service road. It offers a nice break from the rocks you've been walking over to this point.

It's also along this trail that you'll come to one of the hike's most interesting features. Fifteen yards off the trail at 5.5 miles is Wildcat Spring, where water bubbles to the surface, constantly stirring gentle clouds of sand at the bottom of a pool.

Back on track, climb until 5.8 miles, when you'll turn left onto Shelter Rock Trail. This will take you through the heart of the Mount Davis Natural Area, past laurel, ferns, and sassafras. It's sharply uphill for a while, though.

The payoff comes at 6.8 miles, when you emerge at the Mount Davis observation tower. Spend a little time here, reading the information plaques and climbing the tower itself for an eagle-eye view of the surrounding country.

A VIOLENT HISTORY

The Mount Davis area is a place with a wild, sometimes violent, history. It sits atop Negro Mountain, so called because a large, powerfully built black man fought ferociously here before being killed by Indians.

A nearby area called Baughman Rocks memorializes the place where an ill-tempered father struck his youngest son with a stick. Thinking him dead, he left the boy. Although the boy's body disappeared and was never found, the father was convicted of murder.

This is also where a young girl named Lydia Shultz got lost in the woods. She survived months on her own—sometimes hiding from the very people searching for her—and had gone "wild" by the time she was found.

Plaques located near the picnic area and at the base of the observation tower near Mount Davis provide more details about all of these characters.

A fallen tree along Tub Mill Trail at Mount Davis.

When you're ready to move on, follow High Point Trail. It will wind through a young forest with few trees more than 20 feet high, then gradually move into some bigger timber closer to the picnic area. End the hike back where you started at 7.8 miles.

Miles and Directions

0.0 Park at the Mount Davis Picnic Area. Keeping the restrooms on your left, walk to the right (west) to the trailhead.

0.1 Quickly come to a junction with the Tub Mill Trail. Turn left to follow that path.

1.7 It's hard to see, hidden by boulders and mountain laurel, but you'll cross a small stream here.

2.1 Some rock formations make this section of trail interesting.

2.6 Continue walking and you'll come to a junction with Timberslide Trail. Stay to the left to continue the hike.

2.9 The junction with South Wolf Rock Road means walking a short way on gravel. Turn right and follow the road.

3.4 Leave the gravel road by turning left at the junction with Laurel Run Trail. You'll reenter the woods by some pines.

4.4 Turn right at a junction to follow Wolf Rock Trail.

5.5 Look on the right for Wildcat Spring, which lies just a few steps off the main hike and is worth a look.

5.8 Turn left at the junction with Shelter Rock Trail.

6.8 Come to the High Point observation tower. Climbing up gives you a look at the surrounding countryside.

7.8 Arrive back at the picnic area.

GREEN TIP
**Pack out what you pack in, even food scraps,
because they can attract wild animals.**

20 Mountain Streams

This hike uses a number of trails that are part of the Mountain Streams trail system in Forbes State Forest. Sights along the way include Indian Creek, a very good trout stream (though in places you have to bushwhack to get to it), some regenerating forests that are prime country for black bears, and even a bit of pastoral farm country.

Start: Pike Run parking lot
Distance: 6.7-mile lollipop
Approximate hiking time: 3–3.5 hours
Difficulty: Easy to moderate, with a few hills
Trail surface: Dirt paths and an old railroad bed
Seasons: Year-round
Other trail users: Cross-country skiers, bicyclists, horseback riders, and hunters
Canine compatibility: Dogs permitted; leashes not required

Land status: State forest
Fees and permits: No fees or permits required
Maps: Forest map available by contacting Forbes State Forest; USGS Seven Springs
Trail contacts: Forbes State Forest, Bureau of Forestry, Forestry District #4, PO Box 518, Laughlintown 15655; (724) 238-1200; www .dcnr.state.pa.us/forestry/stateforests/forbes .aspx
Special considerations: This area is open to hunting.

Finding the trailhead: From the Pennsylvania Turnpike, exit at Donegal. Turn left onto Route 31 east. Just past the junction with Route 381 north, pull into the Pike Run parking area on the left. *DeLorme: Pennsylvania Atlas & Gazetteer:* Page 72 D4. Trailhead GPS coordinates: N40 04.756 / W79 19.401

The Hike

This very pleasant hike, without any particularly strenuous climbs, utilizes the Mountain Streams trail system in Forbes State Forest, near Donegal.

This is a hike with ties to the area's industrial past. At one time, several railroads operated in this area, carrying coal and timber out of the Laurel Highlands. You won't find any trains now; those days are gone. The old rail grades still exist, however, as footpaths. One of them forms a major part of this hike.

To begin, start at the Pike Run parking area, which has a sign memorializing Jeff Barr, a mountain biker who spent a lot of time here. The trail hugs the edge of the state forest property, with posted signs to the left. There's a good bit of greenbrier, too, but it's trimmed back and poses no real problems.

The trail intersects a water line right-of-way at 0.3 mile. Cross straight over it and you'll come to two bridges around 0.5 mile. Both span creekbeds that are dry as often as not, but they make the walking easy anyway.

Reflections in Indian Creek. ▶

The walking along Blair Brothers Railroad Grade is flat and easy.

There's another bridge at 0.7 mile. Mile 0.8 brings you to a junction with Camp Run Road. Cross straight over the road, keeping an eye out for black bears. There's been some timbering here, and the resulting piles of limbs make perfect denning cover for hibernating bruins. I've often see bear sign here but never been lucky enough to see a bear itself—though the district forester, Ed Callahan, tells me he has seen bears not once but twice.

The trail turns left away from this cut at 1.0 mile. Cross an unnamed dirt road at 1.2 miles and then go around a gate, following the red blazes.

You'll next come to a T in the trail at 1.3 miles. Turn left, following the signs for Camp Run Road and the Blair Brothers Railroad grade. The trail here is a flat and easy, making it popular with horseback riders. You'll follow this for about 0.3 mile, then, before crossing Route 381, turn left toward a gate. This leads to a parking area. Go around the gate, cross the parking area, and pick up the Dan Carns Trail at 1.9 miles.

Crossing another footbridge takes you into a young woods thick with crabapples. Climb a hill, then descend into another area that looks as if it was cut not too long ago.

At 2.3 miles you'll go around another gate into a grassy opening. Drop down to Route 381, cross the road bridge there, then turn right into the woods on what is the old Blair Brothers Railroad grade. You're along Indian Creek, another fine trout

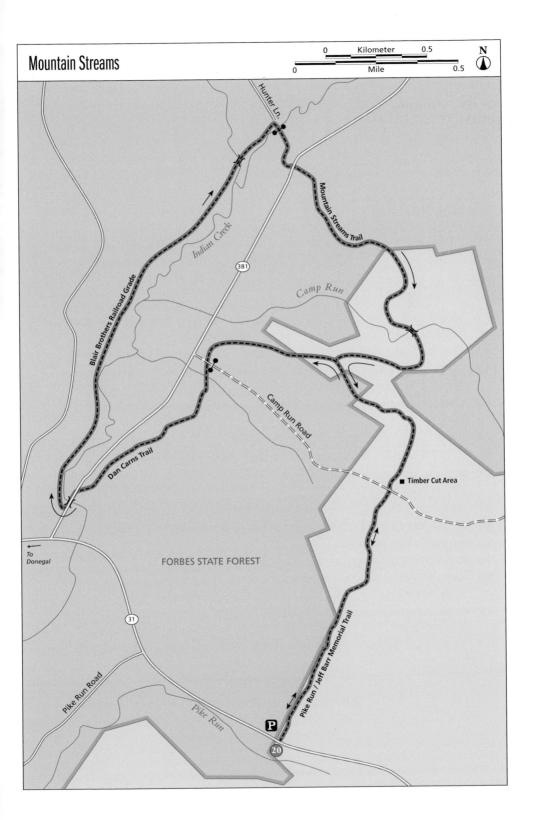

Mountain Streams

0 Kilometer 0.5
0 Mile 0.5

N

Hunter Ln.

Mountain Streams Trail

Indian Creek

381

Camp Run

Blair Brothers Railroad Grade

Camp Run Road

Dan Carns Trail

■ Timber Cut Area

To Donegal

FORBES STATE FOREST

Pike Run / Jeff Barr Memorial Trail

31

Pike Run Road

Pike Run

P

20

stream that's open to fishing only with artificial lures. There's some shagbark hickory here, so expect to see squirrels feasting on nuts.

Mile 3.0 brings you to a Y with red blazes on each branch of the trail. Turn left and continue along the railroad grade. The forest canopy opens up on the right at 3.4 miles, site of an old farm field perhaps?

A bridge, this one with water beneath it, shows up at 3.7 miles. Cross it, then at 3.9 miles go around a gate and turn right onto Hunter Lane, a gravel road. Follow the road past a field up to Route 381, cross that road, and reenter the woods on Mountain Streams Trail.

The trail makes a short climb, then Ts. Go right and begin a longer, gentler ascent up a wide, clear path. Cross a bridge over pretty Camp Run at 4.9 miles.

You'll make one last short climb before Mountain Streams Trail comes to a junction with Pike Run Trail at 5.2 miles. Turn left to return to the starting point.

Miles and Directions

0.0 Begin at the Pike Run parking lot, which is located on the left side of Route 31 as you're heading east.

0.5 Cross two bridges, both of which span a streambed that's dry as often as not in summer.

0.8 The trail here crosses Camp Run Road, a dirt road through the woods. Continue straight, keeping a cut area on your right.

1.3 At an unmarked trail junction, turn left toward Camp Run Road/Blair Brothers Railroad grade.

1.6 The trail Ys. Turn left to head for the Dan Carns Trail.

2.3 The trail empties into a small field. Cross the field and then cross Route 381.

3.0 At an unmarked Y, go left onto Blair Brothers Railroad grade. To the right is an angler's path leading to the streamside.

3.7 Cross a small bridge in an area that's open to lots of sunlight.

3.9 The trail brings you to a gate at the junction with Hunter Lane. Go around the gate and turn right to walk up the hill.

4.0 Cross Route 381 and reenter the woods on the far side.

4.9 Here a bridge carries you over Camp Run. It's a pretty spot that sometimes has a soothing, gentle breeze.

5.2 At the junction of Mountain Streams and Pike Run Trails, go left onto Pike Run to return to your starting point.

6.7 Arrive back at the parking area and your vehicle.

GREEN TIP
Borrow, rent, or share gear.

21 Quebec Run Wild Area

There are many beautiful hikes in western Pennsylvania. But perhaps none surpasses this lollipop through the Quebec Run Wild Area on Chestnut Ridge in Fayette County. A wonderful place for primitive camping if you want to backpack, it's also a great place to go for a day hike, with its beautiful Mill and Quebec Runs. Be sure to bring a camera.

Start: The parking lot on Mill Run
Distance: 8.9-mile lollipop
Approximate hiking time: 4–5 hours
Difficulty: Moderate to difficult, with some hills and wet crossings
Trail surface: Dirt and rock paths; some forest roads
Seasons: Year-round; best hiked May to October
Other trail users: Hunters and bicyclists on the roads
Canine compatibility: Dogs permitted; leashes not required
Land status: State forest

Fees and permits: No fees or permits required
Maps: Trail map available by contacting Forbes State Forest; USGS Brownsfield and Bruceton Mills
Trail contacts: Forbes State Forest, Bureau of Forestry, Forestry District #4, PO Box 518, Laughlintown 15655; (724) 238-1200; www .dcnr.state.pa.us/forestry/stateforests/forbes .aspx
Special considerations: This is a beautiful hike at any time of year, but access to the parking area comes via a dirt road that can be very tough to negotiate in winter. It can be very treacherous in wet conditions, too.

Finding the trailhead: Take US Highway 40 east to the Summit Inn and turn right onto Skyline Drive. Go 6.6 miles, pass the fire tower, and turn left onto the dirt Quebec Road. Go 2.5 miles, past the north parking lot, to a T and turn right onto Mill Run Road. Park in the lot on the right just before crossing Mill Run. *DeLorme: Pennsylvania Atlas & Gazetteer:* Page 86 B1. Trailhead GPS coordinates: N39 45.821 / W79 39.819

The Hike

If a dear friend had time for just one hike and asked you to take him somewhere that would showcase the best of what it is that makes the Allegheny Mountains beautiful, you would take him to Quebec Run Wild Area.

Located along the eastern slope of Chestnut Ridge, Quebec Run comprises 7,441 acres. Most of that is third-generation forest, the first two generations having been cut by loggers, most recently in 1940.

This area, though, exhibits all the traits that come to mind when you think of a mountain wilderness: Clear trout streams flowing over rocky beds; hemlocks, rhododendrons, and mountain laurel shading the water; giant rock formations covered in leaf litter and plush moss—this area has it all. It is, quite simply, one of the most beautiful places in western Pennsylvania.

Water pours through a small chute on Quebec Run.

This hike lets you see some of the very best of that natural beauty. Begin at the Mill Run trailhead on Mill Run Road. The trail will roughly parallel this fairly wide stream, and it can be wet in spring and fall with seeps and runoff.

At 1.1 miles, when Mill Run Trail meets Miller Trail, turn left. You'll have to hop or wade a small stream in a few steps.

Mile 1.3 brings you to a junction with Rankin Trail; turn left to stay on Mill Run, crossing the first of many bridges built by the Pennsylvania Conservation Corps (PCC).

An opportunity to see a little history arises at 1.5 miles. A bridge on the left crosses Mill Run and leads to the remains of a gristmill. Cross the bridge to check out the old stone foundation and some other ruins, then backtrack—stopping to take in the view from the bridge—to pick up this loop again.

The hemlock was designated as Pennsylvania's state tree on June 23, 1931. It is said that "the Hemlock was a sturdy ally to the state's first settlers. Many a pioneer family felt better protected from the elements and their enemies inside log cabins made from the patriarch of Pennsylvania's forests."

The Mill Run trailhead in Quebec Run Wild Area.

Look for skunk cabbage growing in this wet bottom, small waterfalls along the stream, and hemlocks leaning over the water, their roots exposed in the undercut bank.

You'll come to a sign directing you to go right to reach West Road and Tebolt Trail. Follow the sign to mile 3.0, where Tebolt Trail goes left. Instead, continue straight to follow West Road. It's a steady, if not overly steep, uphill climb. In another 0.2 mile, at a junction with Tebolt Road, turn right to stay on West Road.

Bypass an unnamed road and come to a junction with Quebec Road at 4.1 miles. Cross the road, jog 30 yards or so uphill to the left, and reenter the woods at a sign for Brocker Trail/West Road. These trails split in just 0.1 mile; turn right onto Brocker.

You'll wind around a hillside that's first pockmarked and then dense with rhododendron and laurel. At 4.8 miles you'll come to a T with the Hess Trail. Turn right to follow Hess, passing some yellow poplars.

You'll hear before you see Quebec Run, smaller than Mill Run but no less spectacular. You'll begin to follow it at 5.8 miles and continue for a little more than 0.5 mile.

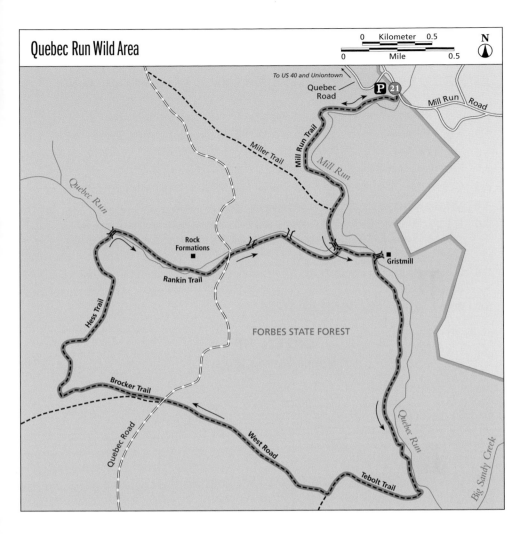

0   Kilometer   0.5

0   Mile   0.5

N

To US 40 and Uniontown

Quebec Road

P 21

Mill Run Road

Mill Run Trail

Miller Trail

Mill Run

Quebec Run

Rock Formations

Rankin Trail

Gristmill

Hess Trail

FORBES STATE FOREST

Brocker Trail

Quebec Road

West Road

Quebec Run

Tebolt Trail

Big Sandy Creek

A bridge carries you over Quebec Run, and at 6.4 miles you'll turn right onto Rankin Trail. The walking is cooler here, winding among hemlocks with Quebec Run on the right—shooting over long, slick rock faces and between boulders half as big as a Volkswagen Beetle—and some rock formations on the left. It's a spectacular stretch of trail.

Cross Quebec Road at 7.1 miles. You'll go over two more PCC bridges and at 7.6 miles come to a junction with Miller Trail. Turn left, walk a few hundred yards, and then turn right onto Mill Run Trail to return to your vehicle.

◀   *A tiny waterfall on Quebec Run.*

Miles and Directions

0.0 Begin at the Mill Run trailhead, a small parking area that can be wet at times.

1.1 This is the first of several trail intersections. Here, at the junction with Miller Trail, turn left onto Mill Run.

1.3 This is the second trail junction, with Rankin Trail. Turn left to remain on Mill Run.

1.5 A spur trail here leads across a bridge over Mill Run to some gristmill ruins. There's not a lot left standing, but what's there is worth a look.

3.0 At the junction with West Road, turn right.

4.1 Cross Quebec Road, turning right onto Brocker Trail, which is marked with a sign.

4.8 Meet up with Hess Trail. Turn right and follow the trail downslope.

6.4 At the junction with Rankin Trail, turn right and walk so that Quebec Run is on your right. This is undoubtedly the most spectacular portion of this hike, given the way Quebec Run pours over some boulders.

7.6 Come to the junction with Miller Trail. Turn left and retrace some of the steps you took earlier.

8.9 Arrive back at the trailhead and your vehicle.

GREEN TIP
Reuse zip-top bags.

22 Roaring Run Natural Area

Roaring Run is a beautiful mountain stream that's been designated as having "exceptional value" by the state. It's a wilderness trout stream, too. But you'll find all of that out if you do this hike, since you'll spend almost as much time in the water as a fish. A significant portion of the walk follows Roaring Run down a deep valley, walled in on both sides by significant slopes, so you will cross the stream many, many times.

Start: The first parking area on Fire Tower Road
Distance: 8.9-mile lollipop
Approximate hiking time: 4–5.5 hours
Difficulty: Moderate to difficult, with numerous wet stream crossings and one significant climb
Trail surface: Dirt paths
Seasons: Year-round; best hiked April to November
Other trail users: Cross-country skiers and hunters
Canine compatibility: Dogs permitted; leashes not required

Land status: State forest
Fees and permits: No fees or permits required
Maps: Forest map available by contacting Forbes State Forest; USGS Seven Springs
Trail contacts: Forbes State Forest, Bureau of Forestry, Forestry District #4, PO Box 518, Laughlintown 15655; (724) 238-1200; www.dcnr.state.pa.us/forestry/stateforests/forbes.aspx
Special considerations: This area is open to hunting. Significant snowfall can make this hike very challenging.

Finding the trailhead: Take the Pennsylvania Turnpike to Donegal and turn left onto Route 31 east. Just before reaching Kooser State Park, turn right onto Fire Tower Road. Park in the first lot on the right. *DeLorme: Pennsylvania Atlas & Gazetteer:* Page 73 D4. Trailhead GPS coordinates: N40 03.988 / W79 16.336

The Hike

It's not true that the majority of the 3,593-acre Roaring Run Natural Area is underwater. But when you look up, see 100 yards of Roaring Run Trail ahead, and notice that the stream crosses the trail four or six or eight times—never with benefit of a bridge, mind you—it can feel like it.

But that's more than OK. The Roaring Run valley is stunning just as it is.

Walled in by steep mountainsides, Roaring Run is an absolutely beautiful stream. Any hike in it is worthwhile, and if you enjoy fishing for native brook trout, you've got all the more reason to come here and bring a rod. Add in the views to be had from Painter Rock Trail and the taste of history you get elsewhere along the trail, and this is a really cool hike.

To get started, leave the parking lot on Fire Tower Road, keeping the adjacent field on your left. Follow the blue blazes of McKenna Trail when it turns right into the woods and continue for 0.4 mile along a flat course.

Some of the Mt. Hope School ruins still visible in the woods.

Turn left at 0.4 mile to angle uphill. You'll pass a house at 0.8 mile and cross under telephone wires at 0.9 mile.

At 1.2 miles turn left onto Hillside Trail. It will double back on itself twice as it drops downhill. At 1.5 miles Hillside Trail intersects Nedrow Trail, a gravel road. Cross the road to stay on Hillside. On the left you'll see the remnants of an old stone foundation, all that remains of Mt. Hope School. The trail markers here turn red.

Continue along this trail until you turn right onto Roaring Run Trail at 2.1 miles. You won't go very far before you notice on the right a number of small waterfalls. None are more than a few inches high, but they're amazing nonetheless as they flow in a series, one after another.

Nedrow Trail comes in from the right at 2.3 miles. Ignore it and turn left to stay on Roaring Run Trail.

This is where the stream crossings begin in earnest. Roaring Run is generally too wide to jump, but you can sometimes find rocks sticking high enough out of the water to help you cross. But with so many crossings to be made—we're talking dozens here—it's best to just plan on getting your feet wet and enjoy the sight and sound of the water gurgling over rocks and under mountain laurel.

> The brook trout—the fish found in Roaring Run—is the only trout species native to Pennsylvania and is the state fish. Although the state record brookie weighed 7 pounds, in mountain streams like this, a "big" fish might be shorter than 6 or 8 inches.

Besides, crossing the stream is not necessarily the toughest part of the hike. At 4.6 miles—at a spot where thoughtless people have left countless beer cans—you'll turn right onto Painter Rock Trail. This trail provides some nice views of Roaring Run valley at a rocky point at 5.0 miles.

To get there, though, you've got to climb steeply. And you'll do it while stepping on and over rocks part of the way, with greenbrier clutching at your feet like hidden gnomes.

At 5.4 miles North Loop Trail meets Painter Rock Trail on the left. Ignore it, make a slight right, and continue on Painter Rock. Pass through a last jumble of rocks and the trail will level off a bit before starting back downhill.

Mile 6.1 brings you to a T; to the left is North Loop Trail again. You'll want to turn right onto McKenna (which isn't marked by name here). You'll go down a wet, rocky wash until the trail Ys at 6.2 miles. Turn left and go uphill, following the red blazes.

Another Y turns up at 6.8 miles. Turn left to stay on McKenna. Bypass an unmarked trail and, at 7.7 miles, intersect Hillside Trail, where you turned previously.

This time, instead of turning right to drop into the valley, go straight, pass under the telephone wires again, and return to your starting point.

Fall leaves and fallen logs paint the ground in Roaring Run Natural Area.

Roaring Run Natural Area

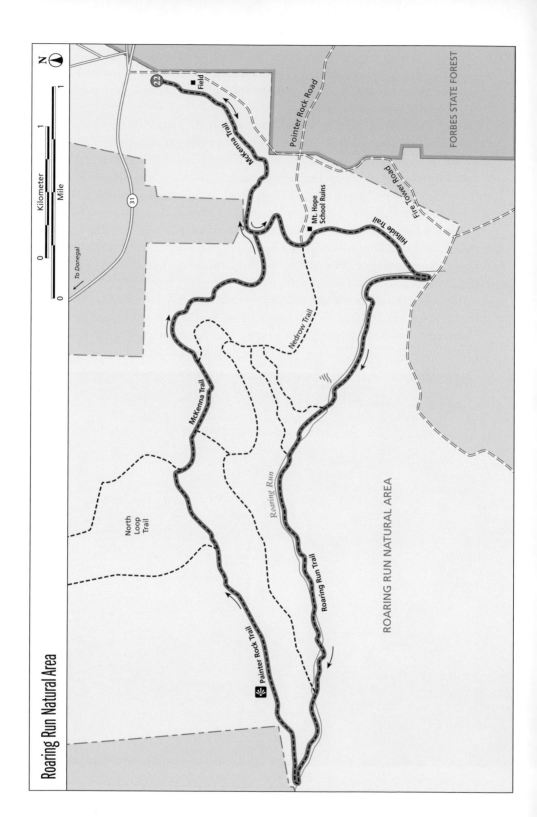

Miles and Directions

0.0   Begin from the Fire Tower Road parking lot, staying right of a field.

0.9   The trail winds below some telephone lines.

1.2   At the junction with Hillside Trail, turn left and backtrack a bit before you head downhill.

2.1   At the junction with Roaring Run Trail, turn right and head downhill once again.

3.1   Look on your right for some tiny waterfalls. They're not big here but are very numerous.

4.6   After having made multiple crossings of Roaring Run, turn right at the junction with Painter Rock Trail and begin a steep climb.

5.0   Come to the Painter Rock overlook. It's not marked, and when the leaves are on the trees it's not overly noticeable, but it's worth looking for.

6.1   At the junction with the North Loop Trail, turn right and walk down a rocky wash.

6.8   Reach a junction with the Nedrow Trail. Turn left here and begin climbing.

7.7   Find yourself at the junction with Hillside Trail that you visited once before. This time go straight and retrace your steps back toward the start.

8.9   Arrive back at the parking lot and your vehicle.

GREEN TIP
Carpool or take public transportation to the trailhead.

23 Charles F. Lewis Natural Area

If you like hiking on wide, flat trails—sort of like sidewalks without the concrete—this is not the hike for you. This hike starts uphill almost immediately and climbs for quite a while. The only part of the walk that's tougher, in fact, is the second half, which involves coming back down. Then you have to step from one upturned, angled rock to another. But there's a lot of wildlife in this area and some wonderful scenery.

Start: The parking lot on Route 403, south of US Highway 22
Distance: 4.4-mile lollipop
Approximate hiking time: 2.5–3 hours
Difficulty: Moderate to difficult, with some steep climbs
Trail surface: Dirt paths; rocky trail sections
Seasons: Year-round
Other trail users: Cross-country skiers in some areas
Canine compatibility: Dogs permitted; leashes not required

Land status: State forest
Fees and permits: No fees or permits required
Maps: Trail map available by contacting Gallitzin State Forest; USGS Vintondale
Trail contacts: Gallitzin State Forest, Bureau of Forestry, Forest District #6, PO Box 506, Ebensburg 15931; (814) 472-1862; www.dcnr.state.pa.us/forestry/stateforests/gallitzin.aspx
Special considerations: This area is open to hunting. The trail is very rocky in places and the area is reportedly home to rattlesnakes, so be careful when walking.

Finding the trailhead: Follow US 22 east past Armagh to join Route 403 south. Go 4.3 miles and look for a parking area on the left. *DeLorme: Pennsylvania Atlas & Gazetteer:* Page 73 A7. Trailhead GPS coordinates: N40 24.687 / W78 59.063

The Hike

The Beatles—John, Paul, George, and Ringo—probably didn't get the idea for their mop haircuts from seeing a porcupine at rest, but they could have.

As I walked up the Clark Run Trail, a noise attracted my attention. It was a porcupine, sitting on a large rock. He froze, then raised his quills until he looked like a puffer fish stranded at high tide. After eyeballing each other for a moment, we began a slow-motion dance. Whenever I would step one way or the other to get a look at his face, he would pirouette, always keeping his prickly back to me. Finally, tired of our two-step, he slowly turned to tuck his vulnerable nose against a tree.

Being in that defensible position calmed him. If I stood still, he would lower his quills until it looked as though one of the Beatles were buried in the ground, with just the top 3 inches of his head showing. If I moved, though, he would raise his quills again with a barely audible swish.

Wooden blocks make a set of stairs on Roger Mountain Trail at Charles F. Lewis Natural Area.

A waterfall on Clark Run in Charles F. Lewis Natural Area.

It's the possibility of experiencing those kinds of things that makes the 384-acre Charles F. Lewis Natural Area, a part of Gallitzin State Forest, such a fascinating place.

To begin this hike, cross a small picnic area by the parking lot and follow the yellow blazes for the Clark Run Trail. It will challenge you right away. The trail climbs steeply up a gorge, the water of Clark Run sometimes visible and sometimes tinkling along, audible but out of sight below rocks, to your left. There's a lot of beech here, with one old tree particularly noticeable because of all the initials carved into it over the years.

Just beyond 0.7 mile you'll come to a junction with the red-blazed Rager Mountain Trail. Turn right, go about 10 yards, and then turn left up a set of rotting log steps

The porcupine is North America's second-largest rodent; only the beaver is bigger. Adult males can reach 30 inches in length, with a 6- to 10-inch tail. They weigh between 9 and 15 pounds on average but can get as heavy as 20 pounds. Females are slightly smaller.

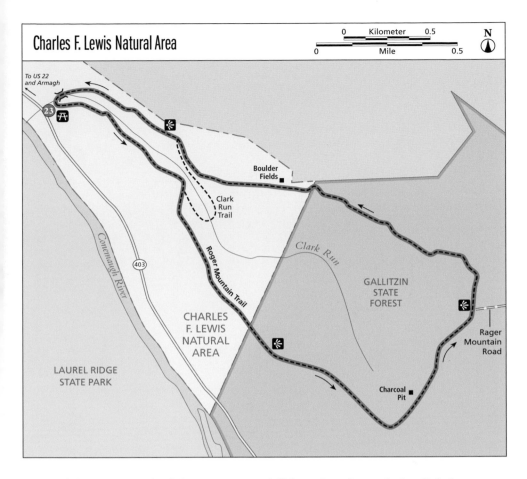

Charles F. Lewis Natural Area

To US 22
and Armagh

23

Boulder
Fields

Clark
Run
Trail

Roger Mountain Trail

Clark Run

Conemaugh River

403

GALLITZIN
STATE
FOREST

CHARLES
F. LEWIS
NATURAL
AREA

Rager
Mountain
Road

LAUREL RIDGE
STATE PARK

Charcoal
Pit

to follow Rager. This hike continues uphill here, but the grade is a little less severe and the trail is a bit wider.

Mile 1.4 brings you to a power line that serves as the border of the natural area and Gallitzin State Forest. Cross this power line and begin to climb again. You'll find yourself hiking the knife's edge of the ridge, with good views to your left.

Some interesting rock formations appear at 1.6 miles. Cross a footbridge at 1.8 miles and then almost immediately cross straight over a forest road.

Rager Mountain Road is reached at 2.0 miles. Cross this road, too, and then over the power line again at 2.2 miles. Pass through some greenbrier, and at 2.5 miles you'll come to another road. Turn right onto it, then left a few steps farther on to stay on the trail. It's much gentler here, the trail winding downhill through a forest of oak, cherry, and beech.

Mile 3.6 brings you to a T junction with the Clark Run Trail (there's a gate visible to the right). Cross straight over this trail and begin following the yellow markers of the Clark Run Trail again.

The trail meanders through boulders, strewn throughout the woods like enormous, irregularly shaped marbles from a children's game. There are cliff faces to the right of the trail. It's all beautiful, although you have to be careful not to twist an ankle.

When you reach the 4.0-mile mark, the trail begins its descent. You can catch a few glimpses of the Conemaugh River, especially if you leave the trail to stand beneath the power line at 4.1 miles.

The trail twists around the face of the mountain, following a somewhat treacherous path of yellow blazes painted on rocks as often as trees. Ultimately it drops to level ground again. Turn left, cross an old bridge abutment at 4.3 miles, and double back to climb the hill that leads back to the parking area.

Miles and Directions

0.0　The trailhead begins at the back end of the parking area. A sign at a split-rail fence points the way.

0.7　At the junction with the Rager Mountain Trail, turn right, take a few steps, then climb a bank to the left. Some log steps make the going a little easier.

1.4　This is an opportunity to get a little sun as you cross a power line.

1.8　Look on your left for the remains of an old charcoal pit.

2.0　Cross Rager Mountain Road here. A "you are here"–style sign on the far side of the road lets you know where you are.

2.2　Recross the power line again as you head back toward the parking area.

3.6　The hike rejoins Clark Run Trail and passes through an extensive boulder field. The walking is tricky here, but the scenery is eerily beautiful.

4.1　At a point where the trail circles back on itself, it brushes up against a power line. You won't cross the power line, but it does offer a glimpse of the Conemaugh River.

4.3　Crossing an old bridge here takes you back to the short section of trail that you started on.

4.4　Finish the loop back at the parking area.

GREEN TIP
Never let your dog chase wildlife.

◀　*Ice coats the rocks along Clark Run.*

24 Shawnee State Park

This is a relatively moderate hike, although there is one section of steep hills—and you get to pass through at least a portion of it twice. Along the way, though, you'll cross a small stream and later follow its winding path; pass by a cove on 451-acre Shawnee Lake where you're likely to see fish, turtles, and ducks; and perhaps see deer, turkeys, and squirrels.

Start: The parking lot by Picnic Pavilion No. 7
Distance: 5.1-mile double loop
Approximate hiking time: 2.5 hours
Difficulty: Moderate, with a few challenging hills
Trail surface: Dirt paths and snowmobile trail
Seasons: Year-round, but hills easiest to walk April to November
Other trail users: Snowmobiles
Canine compatibility: Leashed dogs permitted
Land status: State park
Fees and permits: No fees or permits required

Maps: Park map available by contacting Shawnee State Park; USGS Schellsburg and Bedford
Trail contacts: Shawnee State Park, 132 State Park Road, Schellsburg 15559-7300; (814) 733-4218; www.dcnr.state.pa.us/stateparks/parks/shawnee.aspx
Special considerations: This area is open to hunting, so you may share the woods with turkey hunters from late April to late May and with deer and small game hunters from October to December.

Finding the trailhead: Shawnee State Park is located on US Highway 30, just west of the Bedford interchange of the Pennsylvania Turnpike and east of Schellsburg. Follow the main road into the park, taking the first two lefts to Pavilion No. 7. *DeLorme: Pennsylvania Atlas & Gazetteer:* Page 74 D2. Trailhead GPS coordinates: N40 02.392 / W78 37.347

The Hike

Shawnee State Park lies in Bedford County, immediately off US 30, a roadway that's as famous as any in the country.

The highway got its start as Forbes Road, named for British Gen. John Forbes. His troops—which included a young officer who would later earn some fame in his own right, namely George Washington—hacked the pathway out of the wilderness on their way to seizing Pittsburgh's Fort Duquesne from the French in 1758. Later the road became Pennsylvania's portion of the Lincoln Highway. The brainchild of Carl Fisher, the man behind Indianapolis Motor Speedway, the Lincoln Highway was the nation's first coast-to-coast highway, stretching from New York to San Francisco.

Evidence of all that history is still to be found around the park, from historic buildings to Lincoln Highway murals painted on the sides of barns.

Trees reflected in the water of Shawnee Lake near the old dam. ▶

A look at Shawnee Lake from the corner of its dam.

Fortunately you can enjoy a nice hike through the park without having to blaze your own trail or contend with speeding race cars. This hike covers 5.1 miles, winding through hardwood forests, up and down some steep hills, past 451-acre Shawnee Lake, and along two unnamed streams.

To begin, park in the lot adjacent to Pavilion No. 7, on the lake's eastern shore. Turn left out of the parking lot and walk 0.2 mile to a gated road on your right. That's Felton Trail.

Turn right onto Felton and start up a slight grade, ignoring two unmarked trails that branch off on the right. A Felton Trail sign that shows up just beyond 0.2 mile will confirm that you're on the right track. The trail here—shared as it is by snowmobiles—is wide, flat, and pleasant.

Shawnee State Park actually has a connection of sorts to Pittsburgh. The white barn, buildings, and houses that sit on an island in the middle of Shawnee Lake serve as the regional park headquarters. The buildings were once owned by John Bowman. A president and chancellor of the University of Pittsburgh, he's credited as the driving force behind construction of the Cathedral of Learning.

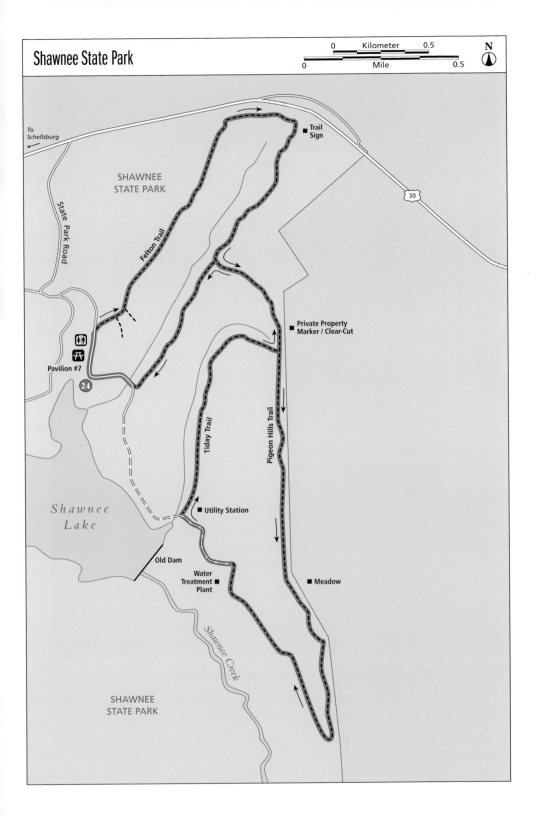

Shawnee State Park

0   Kilometer   0.5
0   Mile   0.5

N

To Schellsburg

SHAWNEE
STATE PARK

State Park Road

Felton Trail

30

Trail
Sign

Private Property
Marker / Clear-Cut

Pavilion #7

24

Tiday Trail

Pigeon Hills Trail

Shawnee
Lake

Utility Station

Old Dam

Water
Treatment
Plant

Meadow

Shawnee Creek

SHAWNEE
STATE PARK

A tree swallow pokes its head out of a nest box in Shawnee State Park.

At 0.7 mile you'll notice that the woods consist of some younger growth, although a few tall, gnarled white oaks still line the trail like stiff, formal sentries. At 1.0 mile Felton Trail makes a 90-degree turn to the right. Follow Felton as it drops steeply down to cross a stream. Climb the opposite bank and, at the sign, turn right, away from US 30, to stay on Felton. The trail follows the side of the hill here, providing some nice views of the valley below.

Mile 1.6 brings you to a Y in the trail. Turn left onto Pigeon Hills Trail and begin an uphill climb. When you crest the ridge, with posted signs around a regenerating clear-cut on your left announcing private property, drop steeply down and then back up again on what is the toughest part of the hike.

At the bottom of the next descent, Tiday Trail—which isn't marked—branches off to your right. Avoid it for now; you'll be coming back out that way.

Pass an open field on your left at 2.1 miles and a patch of crabapples interspersed among some pines at 2.3 miles. It's not uncommon to see deer and turkeys here, so be on the lookout for both.

At 2.5 miles the trail comes to a point where it doubles back on itself to the right. Make this turn, avoiding the posted trails that continue straight and left, until the trail leaves the woods at the park's water treatment plant at 2.8 miles.

Go around the plant to the right. In 0.2 mile you'll get a view of Shawnee Lake, near the dam. Follow the roadway, keeping the lake on your left, to a utility station surrounded by green fence on the right. Turn right onto the unmarked Tiday Trail here.

Tiday follows a small stream uphill for 0.9 mile through another valley, then at 4.1 miles intersects with Pigeon Trail. Turn left, backtracking over Pigeon for 0.5 mile until it connects with Felton. Then, instead of turning right to go back the way you came, turn left and follow Felton in a southwesterly direction. The trail parallels a small, unnamed stream with more doglegs than a king-size kennel.

Mile 4.9 will bring you back to the park road you started on. Turn right onto the road and travel 0.2 mile to reach the parking lot and your starting point.

Miles and Directions

0.0 Begin at the parking lot serving Pavilion No. 7. (Park at the edge closest to the road.)

0.2 Leave the park road and enter the woods on the right at the Felton Trail trailhead.

1.2 You'll know you're on the right track when you pass a Felton Trail sign.

1.6 Here you are close enough to the road to hear traffic. Pigeon Trail turns away 90 degrees to the left. Turn and follow it uphill.

2.8 The trail winds around the park's water treatment plant, which will be on your left.

3.0 Look to the left here and you'll see Shawnee Lake Dam. A trip to the shore might reveal fish, ducks, and mussels.

3.2 Keep an eye out on the right for a small gated utility station. There's no sign, but Tiday Trail starts here. Follow it uphill.

4.6 Rejoin Felton Trail by turning left at the junction. You'll find a small, unnamed stream on your right.

5.1 Finish up back at the parking lot.

25 New Florence

This hike follows roads for its entire length, but don't let that fool you. It is challenging. Only the middle portion of this hike, covering less than 2.0 miles, is even remotely flat. The rest of the time you're climbing—to the tune of roughly 1,000 feet in elevation. You'll have the chance to see some interesting wildlife along the way, though, along with a pretty stream winding through rhododendron and an old iron furnace.

Start: The game lands parking lot on Game Lands Road
Distance: 8.8-mile loop
Approximate hiking time: 4.5–5.5 hours
Difficulty: Moderate to difficult, with some long, steep climbing
Trail surface: Dirt roads and grassy lanes
Seasons: Best hiked May to October
Other trail users: Snowmobiles, horseback riders, and hunters
Canine compatibility: Dogs permitted; leashes not required
Land status: State game lands
Fees and permits: No fees or permits required
Schedule: Game lands open year-round, but this land was bought and is maintained using money from the sale of hunting licenses, so hunters have first use of the land. If you're planning to come here with an organized group, you need approval from the Pennsylvania Game Commission beforehand, particularly at certain times of year.
Maps: A map of State Game Lands 42, and a listing of game lands regulations, can be found at www.pgc.pa.gov/HuntTrap/StateGame Lands/Pages/default.aspx. USGS Rachelwood
Trail contacts: Pennsylvania Game Commission, Southwest Region, 4820 Route 711, Bolivar 15923; (724) 238-9523; www.pgc .state.pa.us
Special considerations: This area is very popular with hunters, primarily from October through late January and again from late April to late May. If you want to hike here at those times of year, it's best to do so on Sunday, when most hunting is prohibited.

Finding the trailhead: Take US Highway 30 east to Ligonier, then go north on Route 711 to New Florence. Turn right onto Furnace Lane, go 1 mile, then turn right onto Game Lands Road. Pass an old iron furnace and park by the gate. *DeLorme: Pennsylvania Atlas & Gazetteer:* Page 73 B6. Trailhead GPS coordinates: N40 21.535 / W79 03.204

The Hike

Doughnuts. Honey buns, cinnamon rolls, and éclairs. And Pop-Tarts. Those are all things wildlife conservation officers typically use to bait traps when they want to catch "nuisance" black bears—animals that hang out around homes, schools, restaurants, farms, and the like, raiding dumpsters, pillaging crop fields, and generally getting into trouble with people.

When officers catch those bears, one of the places they ultimately set them free is State Game Lands 42. Located in the Laurel Mountains, it's big enough—at nearly

The trail through State Game Lands 42 in New Florence will take hikers past traps used to catch and move bears causing trouble around people.

15,000 acres—to give the bears room to roam without causing problems for humans and ultimately themselves.

There's no guarantee you'll see a bear here, of course, but you may get to see the traps conservation officers use to catch them. Essentially sections of culvert pipe with trap doors on wheels, they are often stored here.

To begin, walk around the gate at the parking area and follow the road uphill past a garage. You'll notice a bridge over Baldwin Creek to your left; bypass it—you'll return that way.

Continue straight, following the road until it Ys at 0.3 mile by the New Florence Reservoir. Turn right and follow the orange diamond-shaped markers for the snowmobile trail. You'll come to what remains of the Baldwin Iron Furnace, a still-impressive cone of rock at 0.9 mile. There's a bench here, if you want to take a break.

Mile 1.16 takes you past a regenerating forest and to another Y. Take the left branch and continue following the diamonds. Go left again at 1.5 miles, watching for turkeys here, then cross a bridge over pretty Baldwin Creek at 1.8 miles. At 2.0 miles the trail Ts at a gas line. Turn right, cross another bridge, and follow the road uphill. It

The ruins of the Baldwin Iron Furnace.

gets steep and stays that way for a while. You can encounter snow and fog as you gain elevation, so be prepared.

The trail levels out a bit at 2.6 miles. Ignore a trail that comes in from the left at 3.1 miles and continue past another well at 3.3 miles. Make one more short climb, pass a fence on your left, and at 3.7 miles come to a gate. Turn left onto the dirt road and you're following the Laurel Highlands Hiking Trail north. It shares the road for more than a mile.

Mile 4.9 brings you to a four-way intersection. Turn left, walk 100 yards to a gate across a pipeline right-of-way, then turn right to continue along the road, still following the orange diamonds.

At 5.2 miles the road Ys. Turn left, go around a gate, and walk along a grassy road. You'll pass parking areas on your left at 5.7 and 5.9 miles.

A bench at an overlook at 6.6 miles provides a view of New Florence. From here on, look for Hercules club, a plant with barbed branches. If some of them are broken, that may have been a bear; they love the plant's fruit.

You'll come to a Y at 7.9 miles. Turn right and continue downhill. You'll pass what was a clear-cut—done in 1978, so the woods already look middle-aged—at 8.3 miles, then a field on your left at 8.5 miles. A road comes in from the right; ignore it and continue downhill.

Cross Baldwin Creek at 8.7 miles—remembering to look for bear traps behind the garage here—then turn right to retrace your steps to your vehicle.

◄ *The trail where it parallels Baldwin Creek.*

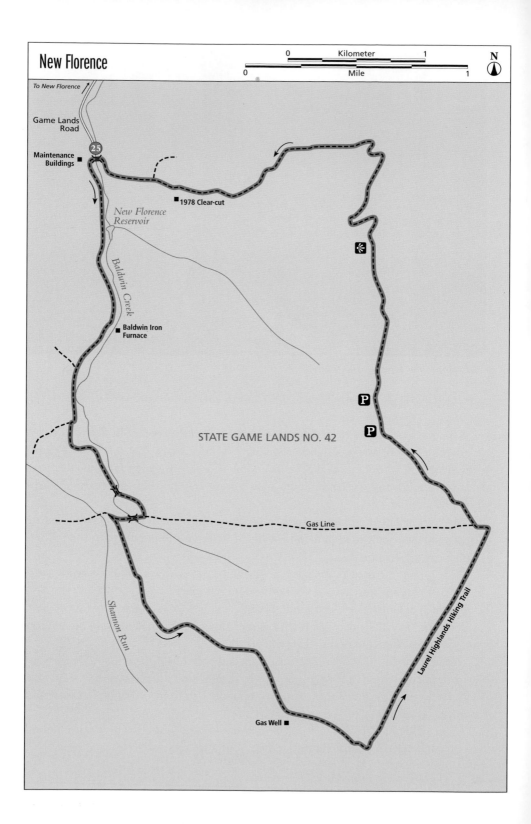

0   Kilometer   1

0   Mile   1

N

To New Florence

Game Lands
Road

25

Maintenance
Buildings

*New Florence
Reservoir*

■ 1978 Clear-cut

Baldwin Creek

■ Baldwin Iron
Furnace

P

P

STATE GAME LANDS NO. 42

Gas Line

Shannon Run

Laurel Highlands Hiking Trail

Gas Well ■

Miles and Directions

0.0 Begin at the parking area at the gated road leading to the Game Commission's maintenance buildings.

0.3 The trail Ys by the New Florence Reservoir; go right, following the orange diamonds for the snowmobile trail up the hill.

0.9 Look over the hill on your left and you'll see the Baldwin Iron Furnace. There's a bench here if you want to sit, or you can scramble down over the bank for a close-up look at the furnace.

1.8 Cross a small bridge over Baldwin Creek, being sure to peek at the stream as it flows out of the laurel.

2.8 A gas well landing creates an opening in the forest.

3.7 At a gate you'll come to the junction with Laurel Highlands Hiking Trail, which follows the road for little more than a mile here. Turn left and follow the road.

4.9 The Trail Ts here. To the right is a gas well; straight ahead is the Laurel Highlands Trail. Ignore both and turn left.

5.2 The road Ys. Follow the left branch, which means walking around a gate.

6.6 You can get a good view of the town of New Florence here, where a bench alongside the trail invites you to stop for a moment.

8.3 A 1978 clear-cut, almost unidentifiable as such to anyone but a trained forester, is marked by a sign explaining why it was made.

8.7 Here, near the end of the hike, you'll cross a bridge over Baldwin Creek. The stream is a pretty one.

8.8 Arrive back at the parking area and your starting point.

26 John P. Saylor Trail

The slightly more rugged of the two loops that make up the John P. Saylor Trail, this hike winds through areas of hardwood forest, across woodland meadows, and along Clear Shade Creek, with some wetland areas mixed in. Fisherman's Path, which you first hike in on, and use again to get out, is fairly steep, but the rest of the hike is relatively easy.

Start: The parking lot on Shade Road
Distance: 5.9-mile loop
Approximate hiking time: 2.5–3.5 hours
Difficulty: Easy to moderate, with a few climbs
Trail surface: Dirt paths
Seasons: Year-round, but can be very wet in spring
Other trail users: Cross-country skiers
Canine compatibility: Dogs permitted; leashes not required
Land status: State forest

Fees and permits: No fees or permits required
Maps: Trail map available by contacting Gallitzin State Forest; USGS Windber and Ogletown
Trail contacts: Gallitzin State Forest, Bureau of Forestry, Forest District #6, PO Box 506, Ebensburg 15931; (814) 472-1862; www.dcnr.state.pa.us/forestry/stateforests/gallitzin.aspx
Special considerations: This area is open to hunting. Shade Road is gravel and can be snow covered in winter.

Finding the trailhead: Go east on Route 56 for 5.7 miles from Windber. Turn south onto Shade Road and go 1.6 miles to a parking lot on the left. *DeLorme: Pennsylvania Atlas & Gazetteer:* Page 74 C2. Trailhead GPS coordinates: N40 11.782 / W78 44.333

The Hike

The John P. Saylor Trail—an 18.0-mile backpacking trail in Gallitzin State Forest, in extreme northeastern Somerset County—is split into two loops.

The larger of the two, which covers about 12.0 miles, is often wet and boggy. The smaller loop—known as the Middle Ridge Loop—will stop you in your tracks a few times, too, as you try to figure out how to keep your boots dry. Still, winding through the nearly 2,800-acre Clear Shade Wild Area, it takes you through an interesting and very pretty mix of woods and meadows.

To begin, follow the yellow-blazed Fisherman's Path—a connector trail—to the Middle Ridge Loop. This trail descends fairly steeply over rocky terrain. You'll have to climb it to get back out, but it's not too bad.

The John P. Saylor Trail is named for a congressman who represented Pennsylvania for twenty-four years. He helped another Pennsylvania native, Howard Zahniser, pass the monumental Wilderness Act of 1964, which has since conserved millions of acres of wilderness nationwide.

A wetland near the Middle Ridge Loop along the John P. Saylor Trail.

At 0.25 mile turn right onto the orange-blazed Middle Ridge Loop. There are also blue blazes here, indicating this is a cross-country ski area.

You'll walk beneath hemlocks, maples, and beech until you turn left at 0.4 mile and cross a suspension bridge. There are orange blazes on the hemlocks here.

Shortly after crossing the bridge, turn left when the trail Ts. The going is a little boggy here, with some ferns growing along the trail's edge.

Cross a tiny trickle of a stream at 0.8 mile; in another 0.1 mile you'll enter the first of several meadows on this hike. Another opening at 1.2 miles sometimes holds grouse and deer. You'll also see witch hazel growing in this area.

Starting at 1.4 miles, the trail next goes uphill for 0.25 mile through a mature forest of oak, cherry, and beech that has an understory of ferns.

By 1.7 miles the trail levels out again. Here the woods often have a lemon-lime, Mountain Dew–colored glow to them because of the yellow tulip poplar leaves and the olive green and white striped trunks of striped maple. Fox scats indicate the presence of that animal.

Cross an old trail at 2.7 miles (a post here says this is mile 3) and walk through some more hardwoods and then a few hemlocks. Mile 3.8 brings you to a shelter with a picnic table and a fire ring on the edge of a grassy meadow. This would not be a bad spot to stop if you're doing an overnight backpack.

NO CAMPING WITHIN 100 FT
OF ANY STREAM OR OPEN
WATER SOURCE

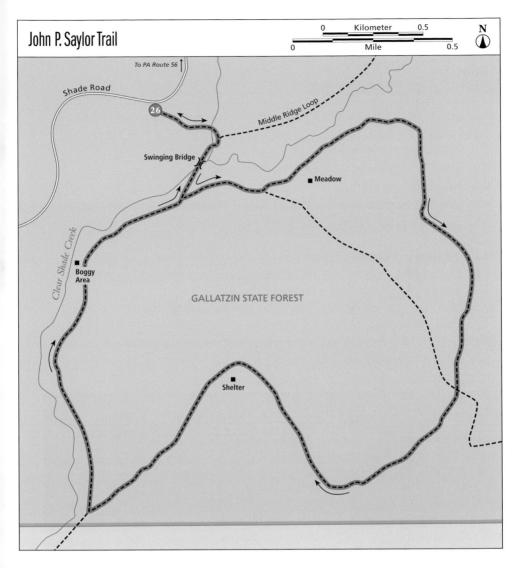

0   Kilometer   0.5

0   Mile   0.5

N

To PA Route 56

Shade Road

26

Middle Ridge Loop

Swinging Bridge

Meadow

Clear Shade Creek

Boggy
Area

GALLATZIN STATE FOREST

Shelter

Across the meadow the trail goes over a tiny stream on a two-log bridge, then comes to a T. Turn right here to double back. You're following Clear Shade Creek again.

You'll need to negotiate another wet spot at 4.5 miles and a seepy, soggy section of trail at 4.8 miles. A low, swampy meadow on the left indicates just how wet this area really is.

You'll get some nice views of Clear Shade Creek at 5.3 miles. If you're thinking of stopping for a little while before leaving the area, this is a nice place to do it.

◀   *Signs remind hikers and backpackers as to where they can and can't set up camp in Gallitzin State Forest.*

Mile 5.4 brings you back to the end of your loop. Turn left here and cross the suspension bridge. Turn right at the T and then left onto Fisherman's Path to return to your vehicle.

Miles and Directions

0.0 Begin at the parking area, which is nothing more than a small turnoff on a gravel road.

0.25 Descend a hill and you'll come to the junction with the Middle Ridge Loop. Turn right here, keeping the stream on your left.

0.4 Turn left at a trail marker and cross a suspension bridge.

0.5 Turn left when the trail Ts.

0.9 Look on your right for a small meadow. It's not uncommon to startle white-tailed deer here.

1.7 Pass through a stand of poplars and striped maples. Notice the distinctive bark on these trees.

2.7 The trail here crosses an old road.

3.8 On your left you'll find a shelter with a picnic table and fire ring. It's a good spot to consider if you'll be backpacking in the area.

4.3 Climb down a hill and the trail Ts. Turn right to keep the stream on your left on your way back to the trailhead.

5.4 Turn left to close the hike's loop and recross the suspension bridge you came in on earlier.

5.9 Return to the parking area and your starting point.

The swinging bridge over Clear Shade Creek.

27 Ohiopyle's Sugarloaf-Baughman Loop

Ohiopyle State Park sees a lot of traffic, especially in the warmer months. Spend time in the vicinity of the Youghiogheny (Yough) River and, with all of the hikers, bikers, rafters, and picnickers, it can be tough to find a place to park. This hike, though, winds through some of the lesser-visited sections of Ohiopyle, where you can still find some solitude, see some wildlife, and enjoy some spectacular scenery.

Start: Middle Yough boater takeout and trailhead
Distance: 7.0-mile loop
Approximate hiking time: 3–4 hours
Difficulty: Moderate to difficult, with some steep climbs
Trail surface: Dirt paths
Seasons: Year-round; best hiked April to November
Other trail users: Snowmobiles, horseback riders, and bikers; hunters in sections
Canine compatibility: Leashed dogs permitted

Land status: State park
Fees and permits: No fees or permits required
Maps: Map available by contacting Ohiopyle State Park; USGS Ohiopyle
Trail contacts: Ohiopyle State Park, PO Box 105, Ohiopyle 15470-0105; (724) 329-8591; www.dcnr.state.pa.us/stateparks/parks/ohio pyle.aspx
Special considerations: Located in the mountains of the Laurel Highlands, this area can get significant snowfall in winter. This portion of the park is also open to hunting.

Finding the trailhead: Take Route 381 south from Normalville to Ohiopyle State Park. Immediately after crossing the Youghiogheny River, turn left for the trailhead parking lot. *DeLorme: Pennsylvania Atlas & Gazetteer:* Page 86 A3. Trailhead GPS coordinates: N39 52.120 / W79 29.211

The Hike

At a little more than 19,000 acres, Ohiopyle is the second-largest state park in Pennsylvania, trailing only Pymatuning—of which two-thirds is underwater.

Still, it wouldn't be fair to say that much of the park is unexplored. It simply gets too many people involved in too many diverse activities for that to be the case.

It is true, though, that some sections of the park are less heavily used than others. This hike, which combines two of Ohiopyle's most difficult trails to form a loop of 7.0 miles, passes through some of those lesser-visited areas. Sugarloaf and Baughman Trails are both steep—Sugarloaf climbs 800 feet—and rocky enough to get your attention in a hurry if you're not in reasonably good shape. The payoff, though, is getting to enjoy what is a truly beautiful yet busy state park without the crowds.

Begin this hike by parking at the Middle Yough boater takeout, near the train station and visitor center. You'll walk it counterclockwise by heading south onto Sugarloaf Trail.

Just shy of 0.2 mile you'll cross a forest road leading to a water tower. Next, at 0.5 mile, you'll come to Sugarloaf Road. Cross it to stay on the trail.

A turkey vulture soars on air currents at Baughman Rocks.

This is where things begin to get a little tougher. At 1.1 miles you can hear but not see Meadow Run—a wonderful trout stream also famous for its natural rock slides that cascade hidden from sight. At 1.9 miles the trail gets steeper yet; it is rocky and often wet with runoff coursing down its center.

The terrain flattens out at 2.7 miles. Here you'll see black blazes indicating a trail that turns sharply to the left to connect with Baughman Trail. Ignore this cutoff (unless you want to shorten your hike considerably) and continue walking along Sugarloaf Trail.

Cross a forest road at 2.9 miles. When you come to Grover Road at 3.4 miles, however, turn left and follow the roadside path for a little more than 0.1 mile.

At this point you'll be at a four-way intersection. Turn right and cross Grover Road to stay on the trail, which parallels Silbaugh Road. Follow the trail until mile 3.9, when it turns left to cross Silbaugh.

After walking another 0.9 mile, you'll come to a Y in the trail. Take the left branch and walk until the trail Ts at 4.1 miles. Turn left onto Baughman Rocks Trail.

◀ *The path to the Baughman Rocks overlook in Ohiopyle State Park.*

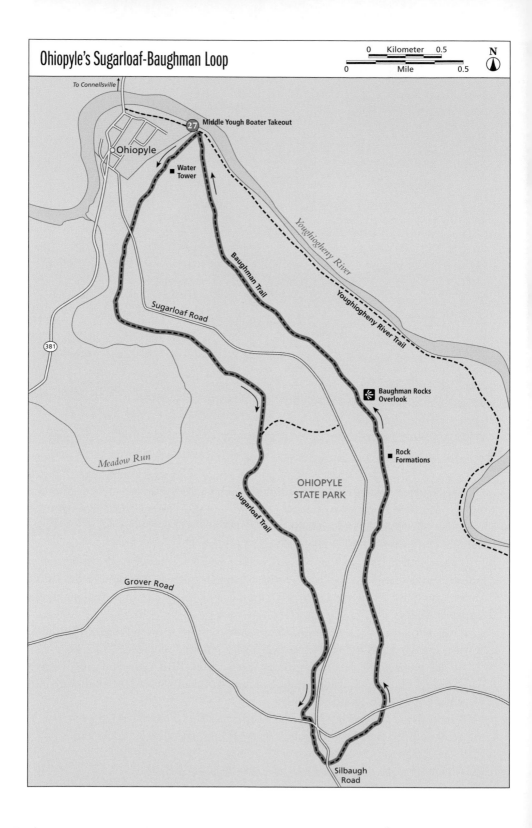

Ohiopyle's Sugarloaf-Baughman Loop

0   Kilometer   0.5

0   Mile   0.5

N

To Connellsville

27 Middle Yough Boater Takeout

Ohiopyle

■ Water Tower

Youghiogheny River

Baughman Trail

Sugarloaf Road

Youghiogheny River Trail

381

Baughman Rocks Overlook

Meadow Run

■ Rock Formations

OHIOPYLE STATE PARK

Sugarloaf Trail

Grover Road

Silbaugh Road

The view from Baughman Rocks overlook.

The early stages of Baughman Trail are thick with greenbrier in many places. Shin high, they'll give you some scratches if you leave the trail's center, so stay tight to the middle if you're wearing shorts.

At 4.7 miles you'll make a short but wind-sucking climb, utilizing a sort of natural staircase at one point, to some interesting rock formations. That's a hint of what's to come.

Mile 5.0 brings you to Baughman Rocks, an overlook with an impressive, sweeping view of the Yough River Gorge. You can see the river itself, and turkey vultures and other raptors are common, wings outspread as they soar above the mountains but below the clouds on currents of air.

Leaving the overlook, the trail widens and oaks and ferns replace the briers. The river finally comes into sight at 6.7 miles. You'll likely hear it—and the hikers and bikers using the Yough River Trail—before you see it.

Ohiopyle State Park takes its name from "ohiopehhle," a Native American word meaning "white, frothy water"—an obvious reference to the park's major waterfall on the Yough River.

You need to make a 90-degree turn to the right at 6.8 miles to stay on Baughman Trail. Watch closely for this. It's marked with red blazes, but because the trail seems to go straight, too, the turnoff is easy to miss.

The trail drops down to the Yough River Trail. Turn left to return to your starting point.

Miles and Directions

0.0 Start this hike at the Middle Yough boater takeout. The trailhead is at the far edge of the lot.

0.5 The trail meets up with Sugarloaf Road. Cross the road and reenter the woods at the sign.

1.1 The Meadow Run water slides are nearby. You can't see them from here, but if you listen on a weekend, you may hear the yells and laughs of picnickers riding the slides.

2.7 Look on the left and you'll see the Baughman Rocks connector trail. Ignore it and continue along the way you've been going.

3.4 The trail meets with Grover Road. Turn left and follow the well-worn path in the grass along the road's edge.

4.1 Meet the junction with the Baughman Rocks Trail. Turn left and follow Baughman Rocks.

5.0 The Baughman Rocks overlook is on your right. It offers a panoramic view of the surrounding country.

6.8 As you're walking along a bench, the trail turns sharply right to descend to the Yough River Trail. It's marked with red blazes, but it still pays to keep an eye out for the turn here.

7.0 Wind up back at the parking area.

28 Ohiopyle's Ferncliff Peninsula

This hike winds its way through the Ohiopyle that is so well known to so many people. You'll explore Ferncliff Natural Area, a 100-acre peninsula that's a National Natural Landmark. You'll likely see kayakers and rafters tackle rapids, get a bird's-eye view of the Youghiogheny (Yough) River from an old railroad bridge, and wander almost under the 30-foot Cucumber Falls. Chances are you'll run into other hikers, too, even on weekdays, but the sheer beauty of this place will leave you willing to share.

Start: The Ferncliff Natural Area parking lot

Distance: 4.7-mile loop

Approximate hiking time: 2.5–3 hours

Difficulty: Easy to moderate, traversing generally flat terrain

Trail surface: Dirt and rock paths, with a short road section

Seasons: Year-round; best hiked April to October

Other trail users: Bicyclists in some sections

Canine compatibility: Leashed dogs permitted

Land status: State park

Fees and permits: No fees or permits required

Maps: Map available by contacting Ohiopyle State Park; USGS Fort Necessity and Ohiopyle

Trail contacts: Ohiopyle State Park, PO Box 105, Ohiopyle 15470-0105; (724) 329-8591; www.dcnr.state.pa.us/stateparks/parks/ohiopyle.aspx

Special considerations: Archery hunting is allowed in Ferncliff Natural Area. There are a number of rapids in this section of the Yough, too, so use caution when around the river.

Finding the trailhead: To reach the Ferncliff Natural Area parking area, take Route 381 south of Normalville to Ohiopyle. Turn right into the lot just before crossing over the Yough River. *DeLorme: Pennsylvania Atlas & Gazetteer:* Page 86 A3. Trailhead GPS coordinates: N39 52.311 / W79 29.646

The Hike

The Ferncliff that draws visitors to Ohiopyle State Park these days is not the Ferncliff that drew your grandfather's father there more than a century ago.

In the late 1880s the peninsula that is now the Ferncliff Natural Area was anything but natural. Entrepreneurs eager to make money from tourists traveling in by train turned the area into a Coney Island of sorts. They developed a few walking trails but sank most of their money into building a boardwalk, dance pavilion, ball fields, tennis courts, fountains, and even a hotel.

Those things are all but gone today. You might find remnants of a few old foundations, but Ferncliff has largely returned to its natural state.

It's a unique one, too, notable for its special combination of movement and temperature. The Yough flows north into Pennsylvania here, carrying seeds from Maryland and West Virginia. They get deposited on the peninsula and manage to survive—miles

Whitewater rafters go down the Youghiogheny River near Ferncliff Peninsula.

farther north than would typically be the case—because the river gorge is slightly warmer than the surrounding area.

This hike allows you to traverse the natural area, see this spectacular stretch of river and the famous Ohiopyle Falls up close and from two sides, and sandwich a look at a "bridal veil" falls in between.

Park your car at the bike trail parking area just north of the Yough River on Route 381 and follow Ferncliff Trail into the natural area; black blazes painted on rock mark its progress. Be sure to stay on the trails here; park officials request that to help preserve the surrounding ecosystem.

At 0.4 mile you'll come to a rocky point that offers a good look at Ohiopyle Falls. A second vantage point exists at 0.5 mile.

The trail Ys at 0.7 mile; turn right and follow the trail markers. You'll pass a deer exclosure near mile 1.1 and, just beyond, come to a junction with Fernwood Trail. Turn left to stay on Ferncliff Trail.

Look for downed trees here. They've been sliced to keep the trail open, but their upended, twisted, and tangled root wads still cling to the dirt they were once buried in like the gnarled fingers of ancient men reaching for some treasure.

Visitors to Ohiopyle State Park check out the big falls near the main parking area, along the hike around Ferncliff Peninsula.

OHIOPYLE WATERFALLS

Ohiopyle State Park, with its river and many cold-water streams, is blessed with an abundance of waterfalls. This hike will take you past Ohiopyle Falls and Cucumber Falls, perhaps the two most accessible and so best-known falls.

There are three others worth visiting, too, however. Follow the Meadow Run Trail to see its natural rock water slides and, farther upstream, places where the stream tumbles over long stretches of rock.

Meadow Run also creates a cascading waterfall just a short hike in from the first parking lot on Dinnerbell Road.

Finally, there are waterfalls on both Jonathan and Sugar Runs in the park's northeastern corner. You'll have to walk a bit to reach either falls, but the falls on Jonathan Run, tumbling through mountain laurel near the point where it joins the Yough River, is especially pretty.

The main falls on the Yough River at Ohiopyle is spectacular and gets a lot of attention as a result.

The trail goes downhill next, leading to some incredible rock formations at the 1.5-mile mark. The trail then winds through a grove of hemlocks and an auditorium-like cutout in the terrain.

Follow Ferncliff Trail to the marker explaining the area's significance, then turn left to reach the Yough River Trail. Turn left onto this bike-and-hike trail and follow it across a bridge spanning the Yough River. This is a gorgeous view and well worth a few photos.

At 2.1 miles, immediately after crossing the bridge, turn left onto the Great Gorge Trail. You'll pass through a woods of oak, beech, and hemlock, with lots of wild grapes, too. This is also a great section of trail to see native wildflowers in spring.

Ignore the yellow-blazed trail that goes to the left at 3.3 miles. Instead, continue to follow the Great Gorge Trail until you come to an iron bridge at 3.4 miles. Turn

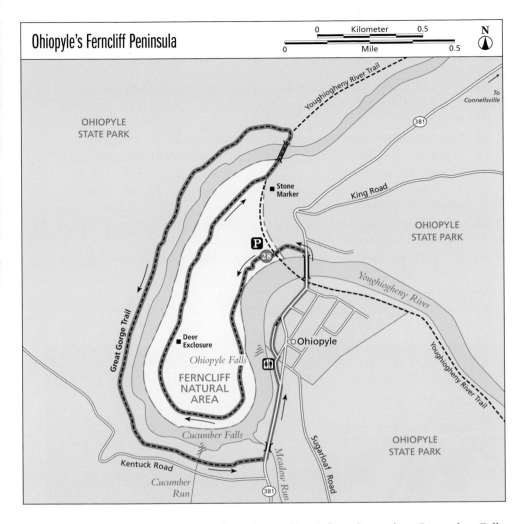

left to cross the bridge, then make an immediate left to descend to Cucumber Falls, where Cucumber Run drops 30 feet over a shelf of stone.

Follow Cucumber Run downstream toward the river for about 0.1 mile, watching for Meadow Run Trail on the right. Turn here and climb around rocks and exposed roots. Watch the river on your left for kayakers floating by anglers and turning to come back for more.

The trail follows very close to the river for a while, then Ys at 3.8 miles. Turn right and walk up the steps to Route 381. Turn left and cross the bridge over Meadow Run and pass a snack bar and souvenir shop, proceeding through the park's main parking area. Along the way you can stop and check out Ohiopyle Falls from this side of the river.

Once through the parking lot, cross the Yough one more time on the Route 381 bridge and return to your car.

Miles and Directions

0.0 Begin at the Ferncliff parking area and trailhead, which is on the left as you pull into the lot.

0.5 On the left you'll find some rock formations offering views of Ohiopyle Falls. From here you can see the falls from the opposite side of the river compared to people who just drive up and park.

1.1 Look on the right for a deer exclosure. The fence will be obvious.

1.5 Walk through some rock formations, which form a sort of prehistoric bowl. It's like being in a mini-stadium of stone.

1.7 As you leave the natural area, you'll find a stone marker explaining Ferncliff's natural and historical significance.

2.1 After crossing a bridge over the Yough River, you'll come to the junction with the Great Gorge Trail. Turn left and follow Great Gorge.

3.4 Look on the left as you descend a set of wooden stairs to see Cucumber Falls, a hidden gem. It doesn't have the power of Ohiopyle Falls, but it's amazing, too.

3.8 At the junction with Meadow Run Trail, turn right to stay on course.

4.7 Finish up back at the parking lot where you began.

Hikers peer down on passing kayakers and rafters on the Youghiogheny River—known locally as the Yough—from the Yough River Trail.

29 Bear Run Nature Reserve

The Western Pennsylvania Conservancy has been buying and saving land in western Pennsylvania for more than seventy-five years. Most of the time, it secures unique and special natural places, then turns them over to agencies like the Department of Conservation and Natural Resources and Pennsylvania Game Commission to maintain. The organization has kept the 5,189-acre Bear Run Nature Reserve to conserve the region's native plants, animals, and their ecosystems. Although the reserve also serves as a monitoring station for biodiversity in the region, it remains open to the public.

Start: The parking lot by the Bear Run Nature Center

Distance: 7.7-mile loop

Approximate hiking time: 3.5–4.5 hours

Difficulty: Moderate to difficult, with some steep climbs

Trail surface: Dirt paths

Seasons: Year-round

Other trail users: Cross-country skiers and backpackers

Canine compatibility: Leashed dogs permitted

Land status: Owned by the Western Pennsylvania Conservancy

Fees and permits: No fees or permits required

Maps: Maps available on-site or by contacting the Western Pennsylvania Conservancy; USGS Mill Run

Trail contacts: Western Pennsylvania Conservancy, 800 Waterfront Drive, Pittsburgh 15222; (412) 288-2777; www.paconserve.org

Special considerations: Only one of the overlooks along this hike is blocked off with fencing. Use care at the others. Hunting is permitted in accordance with Pennsylvania Game Commission regulations, so wear orange clothing during hunting seasons.

Finding the trailhead: Take Route 31 east from the Donegal exit of the Pennsylvania Turnpike. Turn right onto Route 381 south and travel 15.5 miles to the reserve. *DeLorme: Pennsylvania Atlas & Gazetteer:* Page 86 A3. Trailhead GPS coordinates: N39 54.401 / W79 27.574

The Hike

Located on the western slope of Laurel Ridge, Bear Run Nature Reserve faces the Youghiogheny (Yough) River Gorge and Ohiopyle State Park on its northwestern edge, so spectacular scenery is a given here.

There's a lot more to this 5,000-plus acres than just scenery, however. Old-growth hemlocks, rock outcrops, thick patches of rhododendron, even primitive campsites in case you want to turn your hike into a multiple-day affair, make any time spent here interesting.

To begin this hike, start on Tree Trail, located on the northern end of the nature center parking lot. The yellow-blazed trail leads uphill immediately, at one point through a grove of red pines. At 0.1 mile you'll see Pine Trail branching off to the right and Aspen Trail at 0.3 mile; ignore them both and continue on Tree Trail.

Discs mark the trails at Bear Run Nature Reserve.

Make your first turn at 0.4 mile when you come to a Y. Turn left onto Rhododendron Trail—shortened to "Rhodo" on the trail sign—and follow its white blazes.

Stay left on Rhododendron at the junction with Teaberry Trail. The trails here are wide and well maintained, so the walking is easy.

Mile 0.5 brings you to another trail junction, this one with Snowbunny Trail. Turn right to stay on Rhododendron, which begins a steep ascent, gaining 500 feet in altitude. Look for a rock cliff at 0.9 mile and a waterfall partially hidden by rhododendron at 1.0 mile.

At 1.4 miles you'll come to a four-way intersection; turn left onto Tulip Trail. As you walk here, look for sassafras, notable because you can find leaves bearing three different shapes on any individual tree.

Ignore an unmarked trail that comes in from the right at 1.8 miles and stay left on Tulip. Drop back downhill, losing 400 feet of what you gained earlier, to come to a Y at 2.4 miles. Snowbunny comes in from the left; you want to turn right onto Laurel Run Trail.

Turn right to cross a bridge at 2.7 miles and continue along Laurel, following the stream valley. Bear left at 3.1 miles—near a fence post, remnant of an old farm—and walk until the trail intersects Route 381 at mile 3.2. Cross the road, turn right, and

The Bear Run Nature Center peeks out above a split-rail fence.

follow the road uphill for about 50 yards, then turn left to reenter the woods on Laurel Run Trail.

The trail will follow the stream again here for quite a while, until mile 4.0. There a trail to the right leads to Laurel Glen. Stay left on Laurel Run.

Soon you'll notice the Youghiogheny River Gorge to your right. Not long after, at 4.5 miles, the trail splits. To the left is Saddle Trail; continue straight onto Peninsula Trail, which will soon take you past Campsite 4. The trail is rocky here, with lots of grapevines hanging in the woods.

An overlook at 5.8 miles offers a nice view of the Yough. This is a good place to rest up for a minute, too—the next section of trail is a real lung-buster, with a short but steep climb. Finally you'll arrive at Paradise overlook at 6.3 miles. This offers perhaps the best view of the river gorge, as well as the chance to see hawks and turkey vultures soaring on its air currents.

At 6.8 miles the trail brings you to a reverting field. Turn right and follow the woods' edge to stay on Peninsula. The trail becomes a dirt road, leading past an old foundation on the left and then a maintenance building. When you reach Route 381, cross the road and return to your car.

Bear Run Nature Reserve

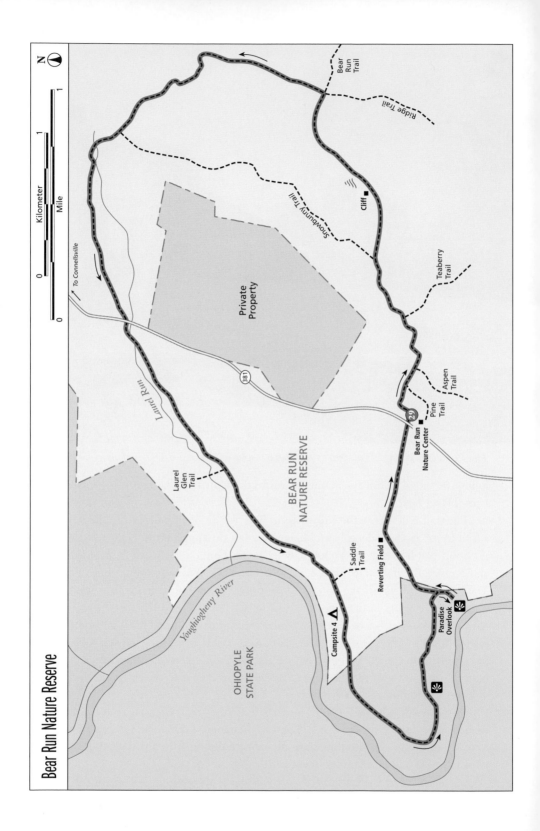

N

Kilometer
0   1

Mile
0   1

To Connellsville

Laurel Run

Private Property

381

BEAR RUN NATURE RESERVE

Laurel Glen Trail

Youghiogheny River

OHIOPYLE STATE PARK

Saddle Trail

Campsite 4

Reverting Field

Bear Run Nature Center

Paradise Overlook

Pine Trail

Aspen Trail

Teaberry Trail

Cliff

Snowbunny Trail

Ridge Trail

Bear Run Trail

Miles and Directions

0.0 Begin at the Bear Run Nature Center. The trailhead is to the left of the nature center as you pull up the driveway.

0.4 At the junction with Rhododendron Trail, turn left to stay on course.

1.0 Look on the left for a small waterfall. It will be partially hidden, but if you can hear it, you can find it.

1.4 Signs mark the intersection of Rhododendron and Tulip Trails. Turn left onto Tulip.

2.4 At the junction with Laurel Run Trail, turn right.

3.2 The trail follows a narrow cut until it meets up with Route 381. Turn right, follow the road uphill, then reenter the woods on the left at a sign.

4.5 Come to the junction with Peninsula Trail. Continue straight to follow Peninsula along the ridgeline.

6.3 Reach Paradise overlook, which offers a view of the Yough River as it cuts through Chestnut Ridge. Watch for soaring raptors here, too.

6.8 The trail will bring you right to the edge of a meadow. Turn right and follow the trail to the field's corner, keeping the meadow on your left.

7.7 Arrive back at Route 381 and, on the other side, the parking area.

FALLINGWATER

You might want to combine a hike at Bear Run Nature Reserve with a visit to nearby Fallingwater. This world-famous home, designed by architect Frank Lloyd Wright, was once voted "the best all-time work of American architecture." Check out the Fallingwater web page for the official museum description: www.fallingwater.org.

The structure's most interesting feature, among many, is the way it extends over and mimics a waterfall.

Fallingwater is open from mid-March through November. There is a fee to get in, and while buying tickets in advance is not required, it's really the way to go. Be aware that no children younger than 6 are permitted on tours. Large handbags are off limits, too. For information, visit www.fallingwater.org or call (724) 329-8501.

Honorable Mentions

Q. Yellow Creek State Park

Dominated by the 750-acre Yellow Creek Lake in Indiana County, this park of the same name is not always thought of as a premier hiking destination. It has two nice, if somewhat short, trails, however. Dam Site Trail is a 2.5-mile loop that leads to a scenic overlook at the dam; Ridge Top Trail is a 2.0-mile loop. For information call (724) 357-7913 or visit www.dcnr.state.pa.us/stateparks/parks/yellowcreek.aspx.

R. Laurel Ridge State Park

This park contains the Laurel Highlands Hiking Trail, parts of which you would have walked if you did the State Game Lands 42 and Conemaugh Gap hikes described in this book. Another section of the trail is worth mentioning. The first 6.3 miles, from Ohiopyle State Park north, are the toughest on the trail, with three steep climbs. This section is also among the most popular, getting lots of day hikers and backpackers. It's worth a visit, though, for its overlooks of the Youghiogheny River. For information call (814) 455-3754 or visit www.dcnr.state.pa.us/stateparks/parks/laurelridge.aspx.

S. Prince Gallitzin State Park

Prince Gallitzin State Park in Cambria County contains more than 6,300 acres, yet it often seems to be a forgotten park. It gets visitors—its campgrounds are proof of that—yet it's never overcrowded. The park boasts 12.0 miles of trails, all of which are relatively short, but they can be combined to make longer loops. For information call (814) 674-1000 or visit www.dcnr.state.pa.us/stateparks/parks/princegallitzin.aspx.

T. Blue Knob State Park

Just north of the Pennsylvania Turnpike, also known as Interstate 76, and west of US Highway 220 in Bedford County, Blue Knob is best known for its downhill skiing. It has a number of hiking trails, however. Two of the best are the Mountain View Trail, a difficult 5.0-miler that winds through a wilderness area of the park, and the Lost Turkey Trail, a 26.0-mile trail popular with day hikers and backpackers. For information call (814) 276-3576 or visit www.dcnr.state.pa.us/stateparks/parks/blueknob.aspx.

U. Lick Hollow Area

The area surrounding Lick Hollow State Forest Picnic Area, located just off US Highway 40 south of Uniontown, is the prototypical diamond in the rough. It boasts the Pine Knob overlook, with a great view to the south. At one time a road led to the overlook, but repeated vandalism forced its closure. You can still hike to the overlook, though, on a rugged trail that climbs 1,600 feet in 2.0 miles. It's steep, so pack lots of fluids in summer and warm clothes in winter. For information call (724) 238-1200 or visit www.dcnr.state.pa.us/forestry/stateforests/forbes.aspx.

V. Whitetail Trail

This trail stretches 14.3 miles end to end, or you can break it into two segments. Either way you need to do it as a shuttle. First built in the 1980s, this trail has just recently begun to get more attention and so figures to get better with time. The trail runs from Quebec Run Wild Area to Lick Hollow, passing over a state game lands for part of the way. For information call (724) 238-1200 or visit www.dcnr .state.pa.us/forestry/stateforests/forbes.aspx.

W. North Woods Trail System

This is a multiuse piece of Forbes State Forest. A section of the hiking-only Laurel Highlands Hiking Trail runs through here, but there are also trails for snowmobilers, cross-country skiers, and horseback riders. Hikers can and do use all of those trails as well. There are a number of short loops here and gated roads, so you can make your own hike as substantial as you want. For information call (724) 238-1200 or visit www.dcnr.state.pa.us/forestry/stateforests/forbes.aspx.

X. Linn Run State Park

Located east of Ligonier, just off Route 381, this park contains two short trails worth mentioning. Adams Falls Trail, which begins at a picnic area of the same name, is a 1.0-mile loop past a waterfall and through a woods marked with boulders. Flat Rock Trail, which also begins at the picnic area, leads to a section of Linn Run where the water pours over a flat shelf of rock, creating a natural water slide that's been used by picnickers to cool off for decades. For information call (724) 238-6623 or visit www .dcnr.state.pa.us/stateparks/parks/linnrun.aspx.

Y. Linn Run Trail System

Though there's a state park nearby named Linn Run, these trails are actually managed by Forbes State Forest. The best of the hikes here is Fish Run Trail, which follows a mountain stream. Quarry Trail is also nice, but you have to share it with mountain bikers. For information call (724) 238-1200 or visit www.dcnr.state.pa.us/forestry/stateforests/forbes.aspx.

Z. Blue Hole Creek

Forbes State Forest also maintains some trails through what is known as its Blue Hole Division, named for a deep "blue hole" on the creek. Some of the walking here is on forest trails; at other points it follows gated roads. You can do loops as small as 3.0 miles or as long as 7.0 miles and more. Prepare to encounter lots of water either way. The stream and trail cross paths in many places. For information call (724) 238-1200 or visit www.dcnr.state.pa.us/forestry/stateforests/forbes.aspx.

AA. Fort Necessity

George Washington's first command was not a successful one. Here, where he built a fort out of "necessity," given that he was outnumbered and surrounded by French and Native American forces, he suffered a demoralizing defeat. Visitors to the site today can visit the museum, tour a tavern, and walk the grounds, which boast a number of hiking trails. Call (724) 329-5512 or visit www.nps.gov/fone.

BB. Ghost Town Trail

A 16.0-mile rail trail in Indiana and Cambria Counties, the Ghost Town Trail takes its name from the many communities, since vanished, that once existed along the rail corridor. Only a few remnants of those towns remain, some of them on private property, but you can still experience some history here on a trail that is wide and flat. For information call (814) 472-2110 or (724) 463-8636 or visit www.indiana countyparks.org.

CC. Blacklick Valley Natural Area

Three parcels of land totaling 713 acres make up the Blacklick Valley Natural Area in Indiana County. The Parker Tract is the largest of the three and the only one with developed trails. On its 300 acres you can find 6.0 miles of hiking and cross-country skiing trails. You'll get views of Blacklick Creek, some old foundations, and charcoal flats. For information call (724) 463-8636 or visit www.indianacountyparks.org.

North of Pittsburgh

The northwestern corner of Pennsylvania traces its roots to three pasts, geologically speaking. The extreme western edge of the region—excluding the Lake Erie shoreline—is known as the Northwestern Glaciated Plateau. Immediately to the east is the High Plateau Section. The area closest to Lake Erie is the Eastern Lake Section.

The glaciated plateau has some hills, with elevations ranging from 900 to 2,200 feet. Yet perhaps the dominant feature is the region's long, flat, and broad valleys. The bottoms of those lowlands are often wetlands. Ponds, seeps, and lakes abound, making the area a magnet for waterfowl.

All of that is a result of the underlying bedrock here. It's made up of a variety of sandstones, siltstones, and shales. Those are relatively soft rocks, so the terrain here was easily ground away millennia ago under the pressure of continental glaciers.

To the east is the high plateau region. Elevations range from 980 to 2,360 feet, with the difference between some adjacent points approaching 1,000 feet. It's more typically half that, though.

What's striking about this area is that it's a country of unbroken forests. Allegheny National Forest, the state's only national forest, is here, surrounded by a number of state parks and forests and huge private tracts owned by timber companies. The trees within them are largely the same age. Timbering was one of the dominant industries here at the dawn of the twentieth century, when entire mountainsides were stripped bare. The state bought up those "wastelands" and replanted them, giving us the parks and forests we enjoy today.

The geology of the eastern lake region is, not surprisingly, the result of interactions with Lake Erie, the smallest of the five Great Lakes at 241 miles wide and 57 miles long. Originally the land sloped gently to the lake here. Now it's more an area of bluffs and, around Presque Isle, sand dunes.

Be sure to hike here. Visiting any part of the north—the pothole lake country of the far west, the bigger woods of the high plateau, or the dunes of Erie—allows you to explore a place that feels unlike anything else closer to the city.

◄ *A tourist train passes the Petroleum Center visitor center in Oil Creek State Park.*

30 Maurice K. Goddard State Park

This hike covers 12.0 miles, but because it's a joint biking and hiking trail, it's paved along its entire length and the traveling is pretty easy. There's a lot to see here, too, especially if you enjoy birds. The trail stays close enough to the lake that if you're inclined to try fishing, you can tote a rod and get in a few casts without venturing too far off track.

Start: The bike/hike trail parking lot located southwest of the park office on Lake Wilhelm Road
Distance: 12.0-mile loop
Approximate hiking time: 5–6 hours
Difficulty: Easy—relatively level other than a few short but steep hills
Trail surface: Blacktop
Seasons: Year-round
Other trail users: Bicyclists, snowmobilers on the trail section north of the lake, and cross-country skiers on the trail section south of the lake

Canine compatibility: Leashed dogs permitted
Land status: State park
Fees and permits: No fees or permits required
Maps: Park map available by contacting Maurice K. Goddard State Park; USGS Hadley and New Lebanon
Trail contacts: Maurice K. Goddard State Park, 684 Lake Wilhelm Road, Sandy Lake 16145-8715; (724) 253-4833; www.dcnr.state.pa.us/stateparks/parks/mauricekgoddard.aspx
Special considerations: Portions of this hike run across parkland that's open to hunting.

Finding the trailhead: Take Interstate 79 north from Pittsburgh to exit 34, then head west on Route 358. Bear right onto Carpenters Corner Road, then turn right again onto Lake Wilhelm Road to get to the park. *DeLorme: Pennsylvania Atlas & Gazetteer:* Page 43 A4. Trailhead GPS coordinates: N41 25.580 / W80 08.836

The Hike

Maurice K. Goddard State Park makes maximum use of its resources, much to the benefit of hikers. It comprises 2,856 acres, but most of that—1,860 acres—lies under the surface of Lake Wilhelm, a popular fishery for largemouth bass, muskies, walleyes, and panfish.

As a result, the park is narrow; in places, anyone with a strong arm could stand on the lakeshore and toss a baseball to its outermost boundary. Yet two trails, connected by short walks along two roads, combine to encircle the lake and provide a pleasant 12.0-mile hike.

The hike passes through open fields with bluebirds and pheasants; brushier areas with cardinals, black-capped chickadees, blue jays, and robins; and forested areas with woodpeckers. With all that water, there are lots Canada geese and ducks, too.

You might even see bald eagles here. None are known to nest in the park itself, but they do live in adjacent State Game Lands 270.

A view of Lake Wilhelm from one of the launches off Creek Road.

To start this hike—paved along its entire length—park in the lot just south of the park office on Lake Wilhelm Road. You'll start out on Wilhelm Trail as it follows the north shore of the lake.

The trail winds through an open area, then, at 0.3 mile, drops down a short but steep grade to two bridges. Cross these, continuing past some hawthorn trees. Just beyond the 1.0-mile mark you'll cross a road leading to Boat Launch No. 4.

At 1.4 miles you'll come to the New Vernon Shelter, one of several small huts located around the lake. They are not heated but do offer the chance to sit down, out of any wind and rain, and catch your breath or just relax. There are containers here for garbage and recyclables, too, so don't leave any trash on the trail.

Mile 1.7 will find you winding along the edges of a field usually planted with corn. Another field a short distance farther on is often heavy with milkweed, whose seedpods run thick with sticky white fluid in spring and summer and burst open to send brown seeds supported by downy fluff floating on the wind in fall.

At 2.4 miles you'll enter woods again, with another shelter at 2.8 miles (according to a park mileage post this is the 3.0-mile-mark, so don't be confused). Just beyond 4.0 miles the trail touches the lakeshore where Dugan Run spills into Lake Wilhelm.

Continue on past a pretty cove and a third shelter; at 5.6 miles you'll find yourself at the breast of the dam. Sandy Creek spills out of the lake on the left.

A great blue heron caught standing along the edge of Lake Wilhelm.

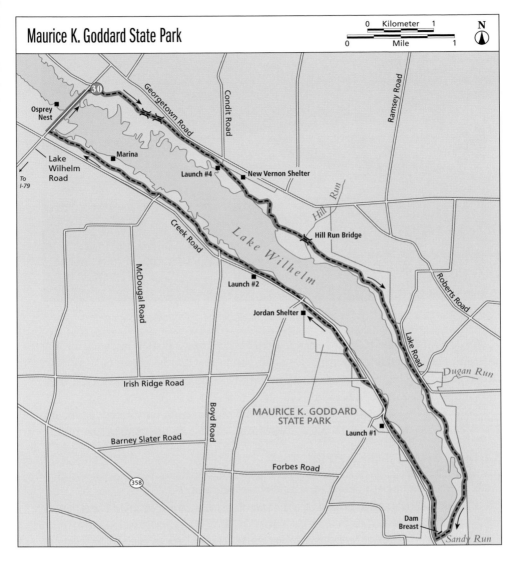

Maurice K. Goddard State Park

Kilometer

Mile

N

Osprey Nest

Georgetown Road

Condit Road

Ramsey Road

Lake Wilhelm Road

To I-79

Marina

Launch #4

New Vernon Shelter

Hill Run

Lake Wilhelm

Creek Road

Hill Run Bridge

McDougal Road

Launch #2

Jordan Shelter

Irish Ridge Road

Roberts Road

Lake Road

Dugan Run

Boyd Road

MAURICE K. GODDARD
STATE PARK

Launch #1

Barney Slater Road

Forbes Road

358

Dam Breast

Sandy Run

Walk across the spillway and you'll see a sign for the Goddard-McKeever Trail leading into the woods on the opposite side of the road. Ignore that and instead turn right and walk along Creek Road for about 1.0 mile. You'll come to Boat Launch No. 1. There—at a spot with restrooms, picnic tables, and grills that would make a nice ending point if you want to make this a shorter shuttle hike—you can pick up the paved trail again.

You'll cross a number of small streams—each of which is identified by name, a nice touch—and climb a couple of short but steep hills.

At 8.0 miles you'll pass a shelter built to look like a log cabin, then drop downhill to recross Creek Road. In time you'll walk through a stand of pines and another picnic area, pass Boat Launch No. 2, and cross several babbling creeks.

Boats, seen behind roses, fill the marina at Lake Wilhelm at M. K. Goddard State Park.

At 10.9 miles you'll reach the park marina. You can rent a boat here, check out the environmental learning center, and see a bat condo that can be pretty busy at dusk. Cross the parking lot to reach the junction with Lake Wilhelm Road, then turn right and face traffic as you walk back to your car.

Don't forget to look in the standing water full of dead crabs on your left as you go. There's an active osprey nest perched atop a platform there and, often, beaver lodges.

Miles and Directions

0.0 Begin at the trailhead parking lot, which is marked with a sign.

1.1 Cross over Long Run, which—like all of the streams to follow—is named on the bridge that goes over it.

1.4 Look on the left for the New Vernon Shelter, the first of several places where you can sit to catch your breath or get out of the rain.

2.9 Cross another bridge, this one over Hill Run.

5.6 The trail brings you out to the dam breast. Cross over the breast and turn right on the far side to follow the road.

7.1 Keep an eye out on your right for the osprey nesting tower located by the bridge over Walker Run.

8.0 On the left is the log cabin-style Jordan Shelter. Built by a local company that makes log homes, it's a unique resting spot.

10.9 On the right is the park marina and education center, obvious for all of the boats nearby.

11.3 The trail Ts with Lake Wilhelm Road. Turn right and follow the road, being sure to stick close to the berm.

12.0 Arrive back at the parking area.

31 Pymatuning State Park

This is a challenging hike, not because it's steep or difficult to follow but because it can be very wet at certain times of the year. The payoff is potentially large, though. You'll see parts of the lakeshore that are rarely visited, perhaps spot a bald eagle or two, and wind up at the famous Linesville Spillway, "where ducks walk on the fishes' backs" for food.

Start: The visitor parking lot of the former Tuttle Campground (closed, but still accessible)
Distance: 8.6 miles out and back
Approximate hiking time: 4 hours
Difficulty: Moderate, with flat terrain but wet conditions
Trail surface: Dirt path and old railroad bed
Seasons: Year-round; best hiked May to October
Other trail users: Snowmobiles
Canine compatibility: Dogs are permitted along the entire length of the trail. If you want to bring your dog along, you'll need to do this hike from the opposite direction. Leashes required.

Land status: State park
Fees and permits: No fees or permits required
Schedule: Access to the parking area is often walk-in only between October 1 and mid-April.
Maps: Park map available by contacting Pymatuning State Park; USGS Linesville
Trail contacts: Pymatuning State Park, 2660 Williamsfield Road, Jamestown 16134; (724) 932-3142; www.dcnr.state.pa.us/stateparks/parks/pymatuning.aspx
Special considerations: This area is open to hunting and is popular with waterfowlers in fall and winter.

Finding the trailhead: The entry to the former Tuttle Campground is located at the junction of North Lake and Fries Roads, north of Route 285 in Espyville. The parking area is 1.25 miles beyond the first gate, which is closed from mid-October to mid-November. *DeLorme: Pennsylvania Atlas & Gazetteer:* Page 28 C2. Trailhead GPS coordinates: N41 38.357 / W80 29.551

The Hike

There are few hikes that are best suited to wearing hip boots, but the one that runs from Pymatuning State Park's Tuttle Campground to the famous spillway in Linesville might be one of them. It's wet, wet, and, in the bad spots, really wet.

The trail is almost completely flat—it parallels the lakeshore, so there's not a single grade to speak of—and more often than not winds its way through open woodlands, with red pines predominating. Yet all that water and, in areas, poison ivy, can make this a challenging hike. So why bother?

Well, park staff and volunteers from a local snowmobile club are working to make the trail better. In the meantime this hike offers the chance to see wildlife like white-tailed deer, red squirrels, and bald eagles—one of the state's densest concentrations of

A gull in mid-flight at the spillway at Pymatuning State Park.

the birds makes its home here—along with portions of the lakefront that few people save boaters ever see.

The real payoff, though, comes at the spillway, where you can buy fish food to throw to carp that congregate by the thousands. Toss a handful of it into the water and the fish splash and fight to swallow it in a slurping, sucking frenzy—all while gulls circle and squawk overhead and ducks and geese literally walk over the backs of the fish to compete for handouts. It's a riot of nature.

To start this hike, park your car in the visitor parking lot at what was the Tuttle Campground, accessible via North Lake Road. It's closed now, a victim of shrinking park budgets. Walk 0.3 mile through the campground, toward what was the 400-block of sites, then turn right (east) toward the remains of Camp Store No. 4. The trail enters the woods at the far end of the cul-de-sac, behind what had been Campsite 420.

The trail is not blazed here, but it's easy enough to follow. At 0.6 mile the trail Ts. Turn right (south) to stay on Tuttle.

In another 100 yards or so, you'll cross a dirt road leading to the lake, then two new bridges built by volunteers. At 1.3 miles you'll cross a second road, then bear left around a utility station to follow another dirt road. This leads to a boat launch and a couple nice views of the lake—and good spots to fish if you've brought along a rod.

◀   *A family feeds gulls and Canada geese at the spillway at Pymatuning State Park. The spot is famous as the place where "the ducks walk on the fishes' backs," because of the amazing number of carp and birds that gather to eat tossed bread.*

Pymatuning State Park

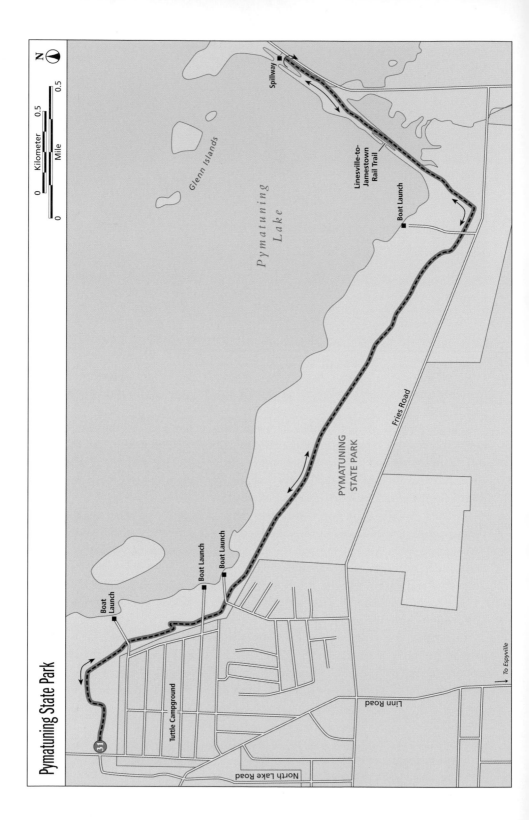

N

0 0.5 Kilometer 0.5
0 Mile 0.5

Boat Launch

Boat Launch

Boat Launch

Tuttle Campground

Glenn Islands

Pymatuning Lake

Spillway

Linesville-to-Jamestown Rail Trail

Boat Launch

PYMATUNING STATE PARK

Fries Road

North Lake Road

Linn Road

To Espyville

31

A pair of black cormorants, one drying its wings, as seem from the spillway at Pymatuning State Park.

When the trail reenters the woods, you'll come across some greenbrier, which makes hugging the drier edges of the trail a little dicey if you've worn shorts, so be prepared to choose between wet feet or scratches. There are some nice views of the lake here, though.

PYMATUNING ATTRACTIONS

If you plan to hike Tuttle Trail, there is another point of interest worth noting.

Walking another 1.3 miles north along the rail trail brings you to the Pennsylvania Fish and Boat Commission's Linesville Fish Culture Station. It's open to self-guided tours from 7:30 a.m. to 3:30 p.m. every day of the year. The best time to go is in early spring, though, a week or so after the ice melts off local lakes. Then you can watch hatchery staff spawn the walleyes that get stocked all across the state. An open house held the first Saturday in April offers games, demonstrations, and other activities. Call (814) 683-4451 for specifics.

By parking a second car at the lot across the street from the hatchery entrance—where the Linesville-to-Jamestown Rail Trail ends—you can turn this into a 5.6-mile shuttle hike.

At 2.6 miles you'll emerge from a forest of red pine to cross a third road, then at 3.0 miles cross a fourth, this one not marked on the park map. Finally, at 3.3 miles you'll leave the woods where Tuttle Trail meets an abandoned rail line that once ran from Linesville to Jamestown. You'll make a 90-degree turn to the left (north) onto this trail. It was recently resurfaced and offers some easy walking, especially after the soggy conditions of Tuttle. It is in the open, though, so sunscreen and a hat are in order.

Follow this trail 1.0 mile to the spillway, where you can cross the road and feed the carp or relax with an ice-cream cone, hot dog, or cold drink at the park's refurbished concession stand.

When you're ready, turn and retrace your steps to Tuttle Campground.

Miles and Directions

0.0 Begin this hike at the visitor parking lot at the former Tuttle Campground, a small lot on the right before the second gated entrance, which is open all year.

0.3 Tuttle Trail enters the woods behind what once was Camp Store No. 4 and Campsite 420.

0.6 The trail intersects Camp Store Trail. Turn right to stay on course.

1.3 Come to a junction with a second dirt road. Cross the road and stay on the trail.

2.6 There's more of the same here. Cross another dirt road, the third one on the trip, to stay on the trail.

3.3 The trail Ts here when it meets up with the Linesville-to-Jamestown Rail Trail. Turn left and follow the rail trail to the spillway.

4.3 Arrive at the spillway at Linesville, where you can feed the carp and get some ice cream. When you're done, retrace your steps back to your starting point.

8.6 Arrive back at the visitor parking lot.

32 Petroleum Center

If you're interested in history, this loop hike through Oil Creek State Park is all that you could ask for. It winds through the area that was the site of the world's first oil well. Numerous remnants of that era—including everything from oil-stained barrels to building foundations to pipelines and old shacks—still remain, left in the woods wherever they fell when the people of the boomtowns gone bust packed up and left overnight.

Start: The office at Oil Creek State Park

Distance: 7.1-mile loop

Approximate hiking time: 3–4 hours

Difficulty: Moderate to difficult, with some steep climbs and drop-offs

Trail surface: Dirt paths and bicycle trail

Seasons: Year-round

Other trail users: None

Canine compatibility: Leashed dogs permitted

Land status: State park

Fees and permits: No fees or permits required

Maps: Map available by contacting Oil Creek State Park; USGS Titusville South and Oil City

Trail contacts: Oil Creek State Park, 305 State Park Road, Oil City 16301-9733; (814) 676-5915; www.dcnr.state.pa.us/stateparks/parks/oilcreek.aspx

Special considerations: Portions of this hike are in areas open to hunting.

Finding the trailhead: Follow Route 8 north from Butler. One mile north of Rouseville, cross the bridge over Oil Creek and make an immediate right near a replica of an oil well. Go 3 miles, cross another bridge, and look for the park office on the left. *DeLorme: Pennsylvania Atlas & Gazetteer:* Page 30 D1. Trailhead GPS coordinates: N41 30.954 / W79 40.845

The Hike

Tombstone, Dodge City, Deadwood, Virginia City—they were wild and woolly towns one and all. Just as bad, if far less well known, was Petroleum Center.

That town sprang up in northwestern Pennsylvania not long after Col. Edwin Drake drilled the world's first oil well in August 1859. His discovery set the region on its ear. Fortune seekers poured in by the thousands, and towns—much like the gold rush towns of the American West—sprang up overnight. The scene was frenzied.

According to the book *Early Days of Oil*, a reporter for the *New York Tribune* visited the area and had this to say: "The excitement attendant on the discovery of this vast source of oil was fully equal to what I saw in California when a large lump of gold was accidentally turned out. When California 49ers came into the valley they claimed conditions here were crazier than any they'd ever seen."

Petroleum Center was perhaps the worst of the boomtowns. It survived only about twenty years, but its short, violent life was marked by countless shootings, brawls, fires, and other episodes of mayhem.

An old oil barrel sits among rusting pipes along Gerard Trail in the Petroleum Center area of Oil Creek State Park.

Today hiking through the park exposes you to some of the ruins from that town and the oil heyday in general.

Start this particular hike at the park office. A hiking trail sign takes you on a path winding uphill. At 0.3 mile you'll come to a junction with the yellow–blazed Gerard

OIL NOTES

There are plenty of opportunities to learn more about Pennsylvania's oil history in this region.

The Drake Well Museum, located adjacent to the park, is run by the Pennsylvania Historical and Museum Commission. The museum contains a full-size replica of the engine and derrick that once stood over this early oil well, along with other exhibits. For information call (814) 827-2797 or visit www.drakewell.org.

The Oil Creek & Titusville Railroad operates an excursion train in the Oil Creek Valley from June through October. Call (814) 676-1733 or visit www.octrr.org for information and reservations for this 26-mile, two-and-a-half-hour round-trip ride through history.

Hiking Trail. Turn left onto this trail, a 36.0-mile path around the park that's well maintained thanks to the efforts of a group of retirees who call themselves "the Over the Hill Gang."

Look for a side trail leading to a scenic overlook on your left and then a red-blazed cross-country ski trail that comes in from the right at 0.9 mile. Bypass that trail and continue following the yellow blazes, which lead to a trailside shelter and a Y at 1.8 miles. Turn left here, again following the yellow blazes, ignoring the white-blazed trail on the right.

The trail meets Russell Corners Road at 2.0 miles. Cross directly over the road, being sure to check out the oil-era ruins found here. Go another 0.6 mile and come to another trail junction; this time you're going to turn left onto a white-blazed connector trail. You'll follow Hemlock Run downhill, cross a bridge, and climb steeply back out of the drainage.

The trail here clings to a steep side hill, then takes you down to cross a working rail line at 3.3 miles. That brings you to a junction with the park's paved bicycle trail. Turn right, cross Oil Creek, and turn left to leave the bike trail.

A trail on the right leads to a parking lot at the historic Pioneer Site. Ignore this and instead turn left to follow Pioneer Run upstream, reaching a T at 3.8 miles. Turn

Oil stains and marks an ancient barrel in Petroleum Center.

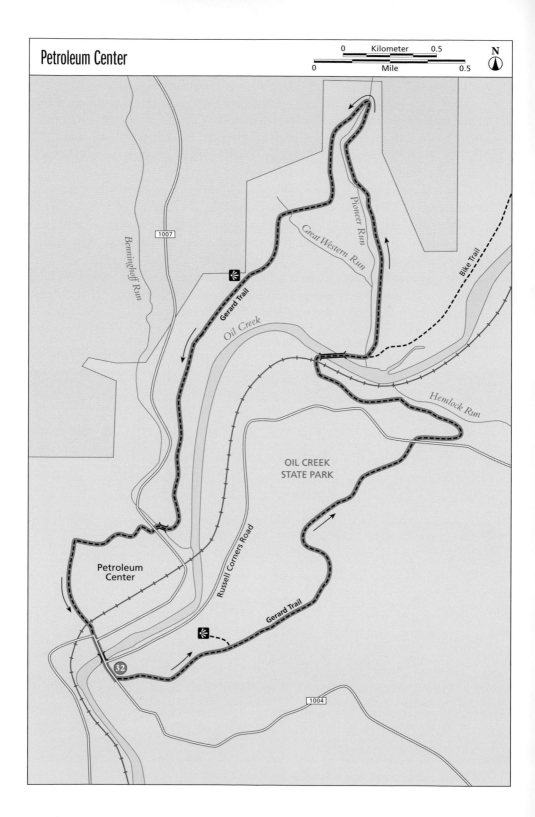

0 Kilometer 0.5

0 Mile 0.5

N

1007

Benninghoff Run

Great Western Run

Pioneer Run

Bike Trail

Gerard Trail

Oil Creek

Hemlock Run

OIL CREEK
STATE PARK

Petroleum
Center

Russell Corners Road

Gerard Trail

32

1004

left onto the Gerard Trail's western leg. Follow Gerard and at 4.2 miles you'll come to Pioneer Falls.

Head downhill, cross a small tributary called Great Western Run, and look for a view across Oil Creek at 5.3 miles. It's all downhill from here, literally.

At the 6.3-mile mark you'll cross a bridge over Benninghoff Run, then go across a paved road. At 6.7 miles the trail meets a dirt road. Turn left and you'll be heading straight into the heart of what was Petroleum Center in its heyday. Interpretive signs explain what went on then.

When you come to a T with the paved road, cross straight over, go across the bridge, and return to the park office.

Miles and Directions

0.0 Begin this hike where the trail enters the woods behind the park office. There's a sign there to mark the spot.

0.3 When you see yellow blazes, you've reached the junction with the Gerard Hiking Trail. Turn left and follow it.

1.8 A small trailside shelter here offers benches to sit on and a chance to get out of any rain.

2.6 Shortly after crossing Russell Corners Road, turn left onto a white-blazed connector trail.

3.3 A working railroad runs through Oil Creek State Park. You'll cross over it here.

3.8 Turn left here at another junction with Gerard Hiking Trail.

4.2 Keep an eye out for Pioneer Falls.

6.3 Cross a small stream, Benninghoff Run, via a small bridge.

6.7 Pass through Petroleum Center, the old oil boomtown. Look for evidence of its existence in the form of ruins.

7.1 Arrive back at the parking area and your starting point.

33 Cook Forest State Park

If you have any appreciation for endurance, you'll enjoy walking this hike, which passes underneath some trees that were already old when George Washington was fighting for American independence. The park's Forest Cathedral is perhaps the best-known example of old-growth forest here, and this hike will take you through the heart of it. You'll also get to see a beautiful section of the wild and scenic Clarion River, too.

Start: The park office parking lot
Distance: 6.7-mile loop
Approximate hiking time: 3–4 hours
Difficulty: Moderate, with steep climbs in some sections
Trail surface: Dirt paths
Seasons: Year-round; some sections challenging if there's much snow
Other trail users: Cross-country skiers
Canine compatibility: Leashed dogs permitted
Land status: State park
Fees and permits: No fees or permits required
Maps: Map available by contacting Cook Forest State Park; USGS Cooksburg

Trail contacts: Cook Forest State Park, PO Box 120, Cooksburg 16217-0120; (814) 744-8407; www.dcnr.state.pa.us/stateparks/parks/cookforest.aspx
Special considerations: Longfellow, Hemlock, and Deer Park Trails and about half the River Trail (from the fire tower to the Clarion River) have yellow and blue blazes to indicate they are part of the Baker and North Country Trails. Most of the trails within the Forest Cathedral are not blazed, although there are trail signs at each junction.

Finding the trailhead: Reach Cook Forest State Park by following Route 66 north from Interstate 80 near Shippenville. Turn onto Route 36 east at Leeper and follow it roughly 7 miles to the park. *DeLorme: Pennsylvania Atlas & Gazetteer:* Page 45 B5. Trailhead GPS coordinates: N41 19.927 / W79 12.544

The Hike

Cook Forest State Park would be remarkable even if you didn't know the history of Pennsylvania's forests. It has some magnificent stands of old-growth trees, including the Longfellow Pine, which at more than 180 feet and 350 years old is the tallest tree in the northeastern United States. The Northeast's tallest hemlock, the Seneca, is also here, towering 146 feet above the forest floor.

It's astounding to think that such trees survived the onslaught of the timber industry at the dawn of the twentieth century. Entire forests were cut, with seemingly every tree bigger than a matchstick chopped down. Fortunately that didn't happen at Cook Forest. First the descendants of John Cook and then the state preserved this island of natural antiquities.

A hiker makes his way through the Forest Cathedral at Cook Forest State Park.

On this hike you can see some of the best of that old-growth forest, while also getting a peek at the lovely emerald-green ribbon that is the Clarion River.

Leave your car at the park office and walk across Route 36 to reach Seneca Trail. This hike will challenge you right away as Seneca Trail climbs steeply up the side of the bluffs overlooking the Clarion River.

At 0.6 mile you'll top out at a junction with Deer Park Trail. Catch your breath, then turn left onto Seneca to walk through mountain laurel and hemlocks.

Mile 0.9 takes you past some restrooms. Stay on the trail until it splits 0.4 mile later. You'll want to turn left. Before you do, though, turn right and walk a little more than 0.1 mile to reach Seneca Point overlook, with its view of the Clarion.

When you return to Seneca Trail, you'll go 100 yards and come to Fire Tower No. 9, which you can climb for a bird's-eye view of the area.

Back on the ground, look for the sign for River Trail and follow it as it switchbacks on its way to the river below, with a multitude of spots good for fishing. At 1.8 miles River and Baker Trail split. Turn right to stay on River Trail, which is actually a gated road at this point. You'll pass some interesting rock formations as you climb to another gate at 2.4 miles. Go around that gate to the left and cross a gravel road to stay on River Trail.

A tangle of fallen but still growing trees presents a colorful mosaic in Cook Forest State Park.

You will come to Fire Tower Road at 2.6 miles. Turn left, walk for 0.2 mile, then turn right onto Mohawk Trail. Mohawk meets Deer Park Trail at 3.2 miles; turn left onto Deer Park.

This trail takes you through boulders and young evergreens before doubling back on itself to meet Route 36 at 4.1 miles. Cross the road and pick up Hemlock Trail, which intersects Route 1015 at 4.5 miles. Cross this road, too, and take the steps down Longfellow Trail.

Cross a bridge over Tom's Run, noting how much cooler it typically is in this stream valley, and turn left onto Tom's Run Trail at 4.7 miles. At 4.9 miles you'll come

The eastern white pine is the only five-needled pine native to Pennsylvania. Cook Forest has twenty-six of these trees in the 160-foot class, three in the 170-foot class, and one in the 180-foot class. How special is that? Only four other white pines in Pennsylvania and sixteen in the rest of the Northeast reach 160 feet. You can't find any in the 170-foot range until you get to Great Smoky Mountains National Park. That makes Cook Forest THE place north of the Smokies to see white pines this tall and ancient.

The fire tower at Cook Forest State Park is no longer used for spotting fires. It is open to visitors on occasion, however.

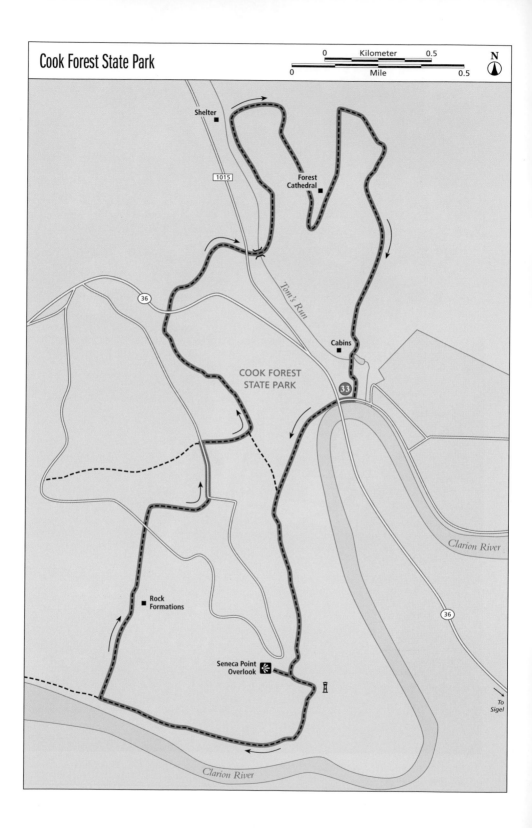

Cook Forest State Park

Kilometer
0   0.5

Mile
0   0.5

N

Shelter

1015

Forest
Cathedral

Tom's Run

Cabins

COOK FOREST
STATE PARK

33

36

Clarion River

Rock
Formations

Seneca Point
Overlook

36

To
Sigel

Clarion River

to a junction with the Red Eft Trail on the right and another bridge on the left leading to Picnic Area No. 1; turn left and head for the picnic area.

You'll come to a T; to the left is the Log Cabin Inn environmental learning center. Turn right, follow Longfellow Trail to a Y, and turn right again, descending into a hollow. Cross a bridge, climb the far bank, and follow the trail as it bends uphill and to the left. This puts you on Ancient Forest Trail.

Walk another 0.15 mile and turn left onto Longfellow. This trail leads to a bench beneath a plaque commemorating this area—known as the Forest Cathedral—as a Registered National Natural Landmark since 1967.

Continue along Longfellow to mile 5.7, when the trail meets Indian Trail. Turn right onto Indian and walk on, ignoring the Joyce Kilmer Trail and Rhododendron Trail when they branch off. You'll begin a long descent until, at 6.6 miles, Indian Trail leaves the woods at the park's cabin area. Turn left, walk past the section of stream dammed for young anglers, and walk the road back to your car.

Miles and Directions

0.0 Leave your vehicle at the park office and start the hike on the opposite side of Route 36, at a sign for Seneca Trail.

1.3 Come to a junction with the trail leading to Seneca Point overlook. Turn right to check out the view, then backtrack to that point.

1.31 A short side trip to a fire tower provides another good opportunity to check out the surrounding countryside. You can climb the steps to get a bird's-eye view of the area.

1.8 At the junction of Baker and River Trails, turn right onto River, which actually takes you uphill and away from the Clarion River. You'll see some neat rock formations, however.

2.6 At the next junction, this one with Fire Tower Road, turn left.

4.1 Cross Route 36 and pick up Hemlock Trail.

4.6 Cross Route 1015 to join Longfellow Trail. This puts you on the path to the Forest Cathedral.

4.9 Follow Tom's Run and you wind up here, at Picnic Pavilion No. 1. It's a good place to have a trailside snack before finishing up.

5.4 Here trees that were sprouting before George Washington was even born make up the Forest Cathedral. A monument to their grandeur marks the spot.

6.3 Leave the forest at the park's cabin area and you're all but done. A bit farther on, turn left and walk the road back to the park office and your car.

6.7 Arrive back at your starting point.

34 Allegheny Gorge

The Kennerdell Tract of Clear Creek State Forest hugs the Allegheny River where it twists and turns through Venango County. This particular hike follows trails that begin on a state game lands and continue through the tract's southernmost section. They're open only to hikers (as opposed to bikers, too), so it's a nice, relatively quiet walk. There's some wonderful scenery, especially in winter when there's snow on the hemlocks, but there are some climbs, too.

Start: The parking lot on State Game Lands 39
Distance: 7.3-mile lollipop
Approximate hiking time: 3.5–4 hours
Difficulty: Moderate to difficult, with some climbing
Trail surface: Dirt paths and old logging roads
Seasons: Year-round
Other trail users: None
Canine compatibility: Dogs permitted; leashes not required
Land status: State forest

Fees and permits: No fees or permits required
Maps: Map available by contacting Clear Creek State Forest; USGS Kennerdell
Trail contacts: Clear Creek State Forest, Bureau of Forestry, Forest District #8, 158 South Second Avenue, Clarion 16214-1904; (814) 226-1901; www.dcnr.state.pa.us/forestry/stateforests/clearcreek.aspx
Special considerations: This area is open to hunting, so wear orange during the spring and fall hunting seasons.

Finding the trailhead: Take Route 8 north from Butler, then exit onto Route 308, heading toward Pearl. Turn right onto Old Route 8, then right again onto Dennison Run Road. Go 1.7 miles and turn right onto Dewoody Road until you reach the Game Commission parking lot. *DeLorme: Pennsylvania Atlas & Gazetteer:* Page 43 B7. Trailhead GPS coordinates: N41 16.119 / W79 52.328

The Hike

Pennsylvania is home to 117 state parks. The forested land along the Allegheny River near Kennerdell is not one of them.

It was supposed to be. The state purchased more than 3,100 acres here in the early 1970s with the idea of creating Allegheny River State Park. Funding ran short, as it so often does, and the site was never developed. In 1980 the idea of a state park was abandoned altogether. Fortunately the state turned the land over to the Bureau of Forestry and made it a part of Clear Creek State Forest.

That won't really make any difference to you on the ground. Forestlands generally don't have the amenities—i.e., restrooms and picnic areas—that most state parks do, but there's nothing lacking in terms of beauty.

Dennison Run in the Allegheny Gorge area of Clear Creek State Forest. ▶

A view of Dennison Run in the area of Clear Creek State Forest known as the Allegheny Gorge.

That's not necessarily what first drew people here. This area was once the site of the nineteenth century's equivalent of heavy industry. Some people farmed locally, then charcoal makers moved in—a stone iron furnace on Bullion Run that was built in the 1840s still remains, as you'll see—and then oil and gas drilling took place. Some of those wells still exist, but that doesn't mean this isn't a pretty hike.

To begin, leave you car at the gate at the State Game Lands 39 parking lot at the end of Dewoody Road. Circle the gate and follow the access road south. You'll come back out this way later.

Mile 0.3 brings you to a sign for the Bullion Run Iron Furnace Trail; turn left here. Cross the game lands/state forest boundary at 1.1 miles.

Just a few steps farther you'll come to a T in the road. Turn right again to stay on Iron Furnace Trail.

Cross a road, and cross a small stream. The trail meets junctions for the South Trail at 1.3 and 1.4 miles. Bear right each time, continuing downhill, to get to Bullion Run Iron Furnace, also known as Cross's Furnace. Between 1843 and 1857, work crews churned out 3 tons of iron per day here, burning 1,200 bushels of charcoal. They stopped production only in summer, when the workers were busy on local farms.

Iron Furnace Trail leads to the ruins if a nineteenth-century iron furnace located along Bullion Run.

The resulting "pigs" of iron—ingots of raw iron that had to be refined in mills—were shipped on timber rafts downriver to Pittsburgh.

When you're ready to move on, climb back up the trail and turn right onto South Trail at a sign pointing toward Kennerdell, at 1.7 miles. You'll pass through an open woods with a few hemlocks and cross a small footbridge.

Make a sharp left onto Kennerdell Trail, heading toward Dennison Point overlook, at 3.1 miles. Look for evidence of old oil pipelines here. Kennerdell will follow the edge of the plateau for a bit until intersecting Overlook Trail at 4.1 miles. Turn right onto Overlook to head for Dennison Point, perched 480 feet above the Allegheny River and overlooking a valley once occupied by the Seneca tribe of the Iroquois Confederacy.

When you're ready to move on, turn right again onto Overlook Trail. You'll descend steeply on a section of zigzagging trail until turning left onto Dennison Run Trail at 5.1 miles. Head upstream, crossing a couple of suspension bridges.

Turn left at the junction with Goat Trail at 5.7 miles to stay on Dennison Run Trail. You'll cross another bridge and get a look at some small waterfalls as you climb, sometimes steeply, out of the gorge.

Allegheny Gorge

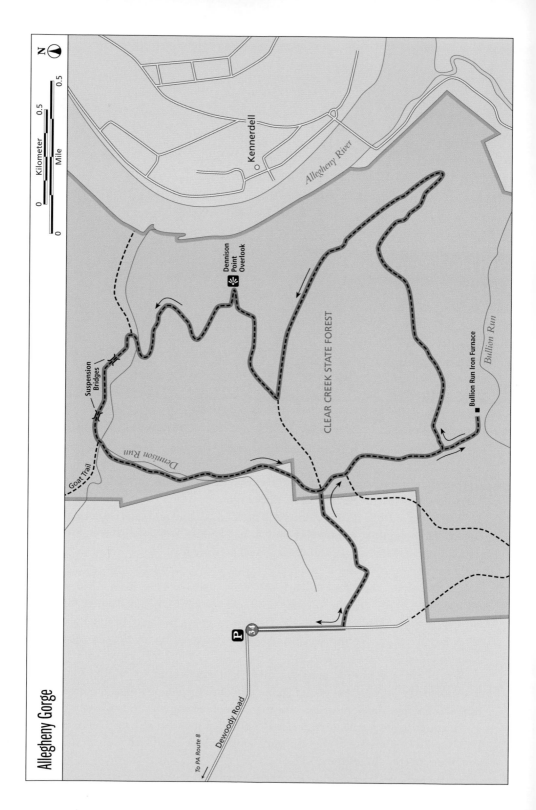

You'll cross back onto game lands property for a few steps. Turn right again onto Iron Furnace Trail to retrace your steps to your car.

Miles and Directions

0.0 Begin this hike at the State Game Lands 39 parking lot off Dewoody Road. The trail begins behind a gate on the south end of the lot.

0.3 Leave the gated road here and make a left onto Iron Furnace Trail.

1.7 On your way back uphill from the iron furnace, turn right onto South Trail. The going begins to get a little easier here.

3.1 Turn left onto Kennerdell Trail. The hike will follow a ridgeline here for a while.

4.1 Turn right onto Overlook Trail.

4.6 This is one of the highlights of this trail. Dennison Point is 480 feet above the Allegheny River, and the observation point here not only offers a great view but also boasts signs that tell of local history.

5.1 Turn left onto the Dennison Run Trail. You'll cross several bridges, then pass several waterfalls that offer good excuses to stop as you climb steeply.

7.3 Arrive back at the parking lot.

35 Presque Isle

This is admittedly the farthest flung hike from Pittsburgh. But it's an easy drive up Interstate 79 and such a unique place that it had to be included in this guide. Walking this hike will not only give you a look at one of the country's largest inland lakes, but it will take you over ground that one hundred years ago was underwater. There's nowhere else in Pennsylvania like it.

Start: The Sidewalk Trail parking lot
Distance: 7.1-mile lollipop
Approximate hiking time: 3.5–4.5 hours
Difficulty: Easy to moderate, with flat terrain but some bugs
Trail surface: Dirt paths, sand, and pavement
Seasons: Year-round; best hiked April to October
Other trail users: Cross-country skiers, bicyclists, and in-line skaters
Canine compatibility: Leashed dogs permitted
Land status: State park
Fees and permits: No fees or permits required

Maps: Map available by contacting Presque Isle State Park; USGS Erie North
Trail contacts: Presque Isle State Park, 301 Peninsula Drive, Suite 1, Erie 16505-2042; (814) 833-7424; www.dcnr.state.pa.us/state parks/parks/presqueisle.aspx
Special considerations: Some parts of this hike wind through areas where ticks have been a problem, so take precautions to ward off Lyme disease. Wear insect repellent for the blackflies and mosquitoes, too. Access to the peninsula can be impacted by snow and ice.

Finding the trailhead: Follow Interstate 79 north to Route 5 west. Go 2 miles on Route 5 and turn right onto Route 832. Follow that road into the park and to the trailhead. *DeLorme: Pennsylvania Atlas & Gazetteer:* Page 27 C5. Trailhead GPS coordinates: N42 09.950 / W80 06.806

The Hike

Like a tiny kite floating in an immense blue sky, Presque Isle State Park is a sandy bit of land with a long, narrow tail that's dwarfed by the inland "sea" around it.

The park—3,200 acres of beaches, picnic areas, and lowland habitat—is actually a peninsula that arches into 10,000-square-mile Lake Erie. That makes it a one-of-a-kind geologic landform. It's also unique in the richness of its flora and fauna. Presque Isle is home to more than 800 species of plants; more than 330 species of birds; and more endangered, threatened, and rare species than any other similarly sized tract of land in Pennsylvania.

Presque Isle is also home to some "new" land. Gull Point, the easternmost edge of the peninsula, didn't exist as recently as 1903. Wind and waves carrying sand from the west have deposited their loads in this area for a century, gradually building the point until today it's 319 acres.

The point is a hotspot for shorebirds, which nest on 67 acres set aside as a natural area and off-limits to human visitation between April 1 and November 30.

The Presque Isle Lighthouse, as seen from the beach.

On this hike you can experience Gull Point while also checking out some of the park's swimming beaches, a historic trail, and a lighthouse.

To begin, park in the lot at the Sidewalk Trail trailhead, opposite the Presque Isle Lighthouse. Sidewalk Trail was originally built by the US Lighthouse Service to connect the Presque Isle Lighthouse and a boathouse in Misery Bay. The trail was a

TOM RIDGE ENVIRONMENTAL CENTER

The gateway to Presque Isle State Park is the Tom Ridge Environmental Center. Named for Erie native and former Pennsylvania governor Tom Ridge, it offers visitors to the park the chance to learn a little about its uniqueness through public nature events, informational kiosks and displays, and school programs. It's even got a 75-foot, 131-step "lighthouse" that you can climb to get a superb view of Presque Isle Bay.

The center is open daily except Thanksgiving, Christmas, and New Year's Day. Hours are 10:00 a.m. to 8:00 p.m. during summer and 10:00 a.m. to 6:00 p.m. the rest of the year. Call (814) 833-7424 or visit http://trecpi.org for more information.

A beach on Lake Erie, right in front of the Presque Isle Lighthouse.

raised wooden platform then. Today it passes Ridge Pond while crossing straight over the peninsula.

Like all the interior trails here, Sidewalk has been a reservoir for ticks. Signs at the trailhead warn you to wear long pants and take other precautions against them.

Follow the trail for 1.3 miles before turning left onto the unnamed multiuse trail that runs alongside the main road through the park. Presque Isle is perhaps the busiest state park in Pennsylvania, and this multiuse trail is very popular in the warmer months, so expect to share it with bicyclists, in-line skaters, joggers, and others.

In another 0.2 mile you'll pass Frys Landing on your right, then a road leading to the local Coast Guard station 0.4 mile farther on.

Mile 2.5 brings you to the junction with Pine Tree Trail and some birch trees on your left. Bypass these and you'll come to Beach No. 10 and Gull Point at 2.7 miles. Turn right into the lot, then right again to backtrack to a kiosk that signals the trailhead of Gull Point Trail. Follow this trail—1.5 miles long—to an observation platform at the edge of the natural area.

On the way you'll pass rare plants like silverwood, American beachgrass, and brook lobelia. You're likely to see any number of birds, too. Waterfowl migrate through in March and from late November to December. Shorebird migration peaks in April and September, while warbler concentrations are densest in May and September.

Hikers and bikers on Sidewalk Trail.

Presque Isle

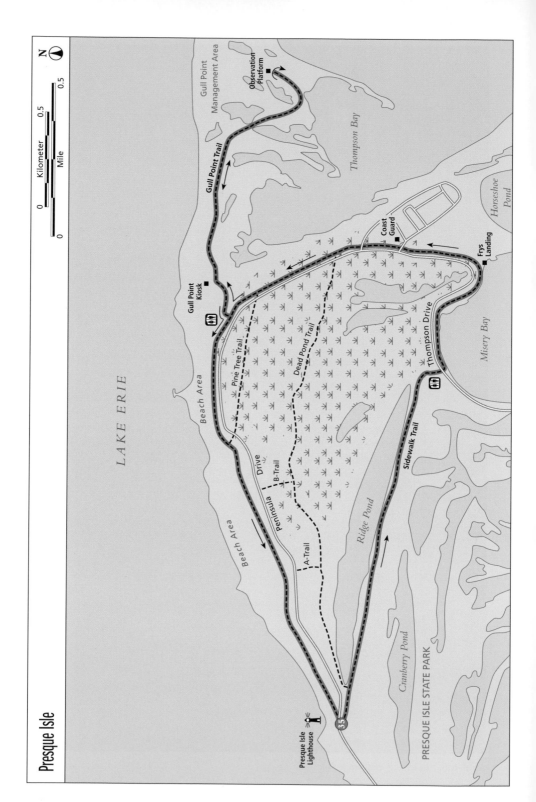

A gull seen from the Gull Point kiosk.

You can pick up a bird checklist in the nature shop at the Tom Ridge Environmental Center to check off the species you see.

When you're done at Gull Point, return to Beach No. 10 and pick up the multiuse trail again. You'll pass some picnic areas, swimming beaches, and water fountains. B-Trail shows up on your left at 6.3 miles; A-Trail comes in at 6.7 miles. Ignore both of these, continuing along the paved trail.

In another 0.4 mile you'll arrive at the lighthouse exhibit and the starting point. Check out the lighthouse from the beach before heading home.

Miles and Directions

0.0 Start at the Sidewalk Trail trailhead, on the far side of the road from the Presque Isle Lighthouse.

1.3 Come to a junction with the road. Turn left here and follow the multiuse trail that runs alongside the road.

1.5 Look for Frys Landing on the right side as you pass.

2.7 Beach No. 10 and Gull Point, site of a one-of-a-kind side trail, will be on the right. The trail to Gull Point begins at a kiosk in a corner of the parking lot.

6.3 On the left you'll see a sign for B-Trail, which leads though an area infamous for its ticks. Stay on the paved trail.

6.7 A-Trail is more of the same, leading into an interesting but buggy part of the park. Again, stay on the paved trail.

7.1 Finish back at the lighthouse and the trailhead for Sidewalk Trail.

Honorable Mentions

DD. Erie National Wildlife Refuge

Headquartered in Guys Mills north of Pittsburgh, the Erie National Wildlife Refuge has four trails. The longest of them, Deer Run Trail, is about 3.0 miles, so these aren't long-distance hikes, but you can combine several with a trip to the visitor center to make a day of exploring this area. Expect to see wildlife, especially birds, at certain times of year. An estimated 237 species live here at least part of the year. For information call (814) 789-3585 or visit www.fws.gov/northeast/erie.

EE. Buzzard Swamp

Despite its name, Buzzard Swamp is neither a swamp nor an evil, brooding place. It's actually a series of man-made ponds designed to provide waterfowl habitat in Allegheny National Forest. It contains 11.2 miles of trail that follow the path of a gated road. You'll be in the open here, so pack sunscreen and water, but you won't have to climb—the maximum elevation change is 50 feet. You can expect to see lots of birds and other wildlife and wildflowers in season. For information call (814) 723-5150 or visit www.fs.fed.us/r9/forests/allegheny.

FF. Minister Creek Trail

If you're going to do much hiking in Allegheny National Forest, you'll eventually end up on Minister Creek Trail. It's one of the most beautiful footpaths anywhere, thanks to its cliffs, rocks, overlooks, streams, and wildflowers. Consider hiking it on a weekday if you can, though, or expect to share it with others, including mountain bikers. For information call (814) 723-5150 or visit www.fs.fed.us/r9/forests/allegheny.

GG. Cornplanter State Forest

Located in western Forest County—the only county in the state without a stop-light—slightly northeast of Pittsburgh, Cornplanter State Forest is home to 6.0 miles of joint hiking and cross-country ski trails. The 1.5-mile self-guiding interpretive Lashure Trail is a good one to walk with children. A portion of this area is also being managed for woodcock, a tiny bird otherwise known as the "timberdoodle," so you may get to see one. For information call (814) 723-0262 or visit www.dcnr.state.pa.us/forestry/stateforests/cornplanter.aspx.

HH. Hickory Creek Wilderness

Covering almost 8,700 acres in northwestern Pennsylvania and completely roadless, the Hickory Creek Wilderness in Allegheny National Forest wasn't always so wild. Where logging camps once churned, clearing the forest, today the Hickory Creek Trail covers about 12.0 miles without any signs of modern industry. The land, a place of ridge plateaus and stream valleys, is returning to its natural state. For information call (814) 723-5150 or visit www.fs.fed.us/r9/forests/allegheny.

Appendix: Clubs and Trail Groups

Allegheny Outdoor Club

This is a group of hikers, bikers, and skiers/snowshoers in northwestern Pennsylvania. Outings are scheduled weekly. For information contact John and Debra Young, 1588 Town Line Road, Russell 16345; (814) 730-2915; or visit www.alleghenyoutdoor club.org.

Audubon Society of Western Pennsylvania

This group not only operates Beechwood Farms Nature Reserve but also leads hikes at the reserve and provides a variety of nature programming. For information contact ASWP, 614 Dorseyville Road, Pittsburgh 15238; (412) 963-6100; or visit www.aswp .org.

Butler Outdoor Club

This group schedules activities ranging from hiking to canoeing to nature skills. Some are run by the club; at other times club members travel together to take part in activities run by state parks, for example. For information contact Butler Outdoor Club, 134 Oak Avenue, Kittanning 16210; e-mail: president@butleroutdoorclub.org; or visit www.butleroutdoorclub.com.

Friends of Raccoon Creek State Park

This group maintains trails in Raccoon Creek State Park and coordinates outings there. It is also affiliated with nearby Hillman State Park. For information visit www .friendsofraccoon.org.

Keystone Ramblers

This hiking organization leads hikes of four types: relaxed hikes of less than 10 miles over moderate ground; hard-core hikes of more than 8 miles requiring a vigorous pace; path-of-progress hikes that explore Pennsylvania's industrial past; and heritage hikes that explore sites of natural or historical significance. For information visit http://keystoneramblersorg.ipage.com/index.htm.

Keystone Trails Association

This is the state's largest hiking organization. It organizes outings and acts as a spokes- man for hiking concerns. For information contact Keystone Trails Association, 101 North Front Street, Harrisburg 17101; (717) 238-7017; e-mail: ktaadmin@verizon .net; or visit www.kta-hike.org.

◀ *Clark Run splits to go around a rock in Charles F. Lewis Natural Area.*

North Country Trail Association

This group, which has several chapters in Pennsylvania, promotes and maintains the section of the North Country Trail that runs across the Keystone State. For general information and details on the various chapters in Pennsylvania, visit https://north countrytrail.org/trail/pennsylvania/.

Rachel Carson Trails Conservancy

This organization promotes and maintains the Rachel Carson and Baker Trails in southwestern Pennsylvania. For information contact Rachel Carson Trails Conservancy Inc., PO Box 35, Warrendale 15086-0035; (412) 475-8881; e-mail: info@rachel carsontrails.org; or visit www.rachelcarsontrails.org.

Regional Trail Corporation

This is the group that takes care of the 43.0-mile northern section of the Youghiogheny River Trail between West Newton and Smithton. For information contact Regional Trail Corporation, 111 Collinsburg Road, West Newton 15089; (724) 872-5586; or visit www.regionltrailcorp.com.

Sierra Club Allegheny Group, Pennsylvania Chapter

This is the closest Sierra Club chapter to Pittsburgh. Members hail from the city and outlying areas and do a lot of hiking in the Laurel Highlands and the areas north of the city. For information contact the Sierra Club Allegheny Group, c/o The Beauty Shoppe, 6101 Penn Avenue, Pittsburgh 15206; (412) 328-9817; or visit www.allegheny sc.org.

Venture Outdoors

A nonprofit organization based in Pittsburgh, Venture Outdoors organizes a whole host of outdoor programs, from guided hikes to kayak trips to fly-fishing classes. There is a fee for most programs, but you get a discount if you become a member. For information contact Venture Outdoors, 304 Forbes Avenue, 2nd Floor, Pittsburgh 15222; (412) 255-0564; or visit www.ventureoutdoors.org.

Western Pennsylvania Conservancy

The conservancy operates Bear Run Nature Reserve and its network of trails. It also purchases property that it then sells to state agencies at below-market prices. A number of state park, forest, and game lands tracts have come into existence this way. For information contact Western Pennsylvania Conservancy, 800 Waterfront Drive, Pittsburgh 15222; (412) 288-2777; or visit www.paconserve.org.

Westmoreland Bird and Nature Club

Though primarily a birding organization, this group does lead hikes, run nature programs, and do other activities that are of interest to people who love the outdoors. For information write Rose Tillmann, Box 188, New Derry 15671; or visit www .wbnc.net.

Hike Index

About the Author

Bob Frye is outdoors editor and manager of everybodyadventures.com, a website focused on outdoor adventure, from hiking and paddling to hunting and fishing and everything in between. He's also the longtime outdoor editor of the *Tribune-Review* newspaper. Both are based in southwestern Pennsylvania.

Frye—writing for newspapers, magazines and books—has won nearly fifty national and state awards for his work. He's been recognized by the Outdoor Writers Association of America, Professional Outdoor Media Association, Pennsylvania Outdoor Writers Association, Pennsylvania Newspaper Association, Society of Professional Journalists, Associated Press Managing Editors, and Press Club of Western Pennsylvania, among others.

Frye lives east of Pittsburgh, in Westmoreland County. From there he explores the state with his wife, Mandy, always looking for new adventures.